THE
Third-Dimensional Man:
CHRIST,
the Anointed One

HE THAT DWELLS IN THE SECRET PLACE
OF THE MOST HIGH SHALL ABIDE UNDER THE
SHADOWS OF THE ALMIGHTY.

PAUL A. BARHAM

ISBN 978-1-64515-364-1 (paperback)
ISBN 978-1-64515-365-8 (digital)

Christian Faith Publishing, Inc.
832 Park Avenue
Meadville, PA 16335
www.christianfaithpublishing.com

Printed in the United States of America

Contents

Introduction

In August 2012, one morning on my way to work, the Lord spoke to me in my spirit and said, *Paul, listen to me. I need for you to understand the third-dimensional man. You are going to minister on the topic.*

Immediately I saw a drawing of an image of a man morphing into three stages. I understood the vision clearly that appeared before me in my spirit but was unable to explain or make sense of what I had seen to tell it to others.

Later, it was revealed to me that the Third-Dimensional Man is the man Christ Jesus in His resurrected and ascended state, and so shall we also be in the rapture to come.

> Behold, I shew you a mystery; We shall not all sleep, but we shall all be changed, in a moment, in the twinkling of an eye, at the last trump: for the trumpet shall sound, and the dead shall be raised incorruptible, and we shall be changed. For this corruptible must put on incorruption, and this mortal must put on immortality. (1 Corinthians 15:51–53)

The second-dimensional man is the born again believers birthed into the kingdom of God, by willingly accepting Jesus Christ as Lord and Savior and the Son of God, who was buried, and raised from the dead. Confession is made of past and present sins; then repentance, a turnaround from sin and shame; and baptism in water and by the Holy Spirit, all by faith in Jesus Christ.

The first-dimensional man, the fallen state of Adam, represents the world in total rebellion against God, striving under God's grace, mercy, and long-sufferings.

> For God, so loved the world that he gave his only begotten son that whosoever believeth in him shall not perish but have everlasting life. (John 3:16)

This book requires you to read it more than once because it provides a detailed look at the fall of Lucifer, and how darkness was established. God sent His only begotten Son in the image and likeness of sinful flesh to destroy the works of darkness and Lucifer,

This book is full of inspiration and words of knowledge that will challenge certain views and concepts pertaining to truth that was never realized but plays a significant role in your everyday life

Chapter 1

My Life's Journey

My Zeal and Pride

God called me to declare and speak His word and make it simple, easy, and understandable, to the best of my ability.

There is a time when I had this tremendous prideful zeal to speak the Word of God. Many of my friends were not able to understand the Bible the way I did and interpret it with such clarity. I was very excited about my faith but insensitive and cared very little to reason with or debate another point of views. I stood firm on my convictions.

Over the years as I learned and became more spiritually aware, I learned to develop more patience and a clearer understanding by studying the Word of God. Because my past conduct was purely religious, and lacking of spiritual maturity and judgement, it did not reflect the fruit of the Holy Spirit.

I was not a good representation of the scripture. My excitement was other people's fear. I was excited about my faith, and it was based on what I was feeling, seeing, and experiencing.

Other believers were not able to feel and experience the zeal that I had for God, which quickly turned into heated debates, and spiraled out of control into an argument, leaving everyone frustrated and bewildered.

With this enthusiasm for God and based upon how I felt, I looked at others wondering, why can't they feel what I am feeling? The more mature I became in the faith, the more I clearly understood that I am not an ordinary believer, and the calling upon my life was different.

Other fellow Christians interpret the word of God differently from how I understand it. I have learned never to judge and make any determination of the faith of others, based on my own personal experience and knowledge of the Word of God.

Now with spiritual maturity, I understand my calling in the faith and the blessings of God and the gifts and callings for my life. Some of these gifts are not sufficiently active because I am not practicing and doing the ministry of Jesus Christ as I should.

However, the most important thing for me was to maintain my faith because in the past, when I had great zeal for God in the deliverance ministry, I was able to see the work of God. Although the power and anointing of God was over my life, pride began to enter into me.

On one particular day in church, in the midst of prayer and worship, I felt this emptiness and unusual feeling. I felt this heaviness when I was lifting my hands to worship God. I prostrated before the Lord and said, "Lord, what's going on?" The Lord said to me, *You have something within you called pride.* It was then revealed to me that everything I was doing meant nothing to God.

I believed I was doing good works in the eyes of God by being involved in all the ministry works and programs seven days a week. My zeal and my pride, along with my beliefs and behavior made me feel very proud of myself, but it brought no glory to God, hence my feeling of emptiness.

Even though I was a part of the kingdom-building process—reaching souls, administering deliverance, giving counsel and spiritual guidance—it was all excellent but unfruitful for my relationship with God.

I took a different look regarding my attitude toward God. I said, I don't want to lose my soul for this. You can be in church, involved in so many different ministries, and don't have a real relationship with God. Nothing else matters but having a relationship with God.

The Prophetic Word from God

I was in the church in the year 2000, and I received this word in Isaiah 49. I had no understanding what this message meant, so I went to my bishop to see if I could get a clear understanding as to what it said.

Verse 2 was more revealing in my spirit:

> And he hath made my mouth like a sharp sword;
> in the shadow of his hand hath he hid me, and
> made me a polished shaft; in his quiver hath he
> hid me.

It was most of Isaiah 49, but this verse stood out the most. As time went on, I began to understand what the prophetic word meant.

The Journey

I got saved when I accepted Jesus Christ as my Lord and Savior. I was baptized in April 1997 and my wife got baptized in May 1997. I developed the zeal from the moment the Lord called me with a distinct voice, and I rolled off my bed, bowed my head, and said, "Lord, here I am."

I developed a zeal for God. My life was transformed in a different way from the norm. I say this because as a child growing up at the age of four, I had a speech impediment making it difficult for me to speak, and to articulate my thoughts. I had a difficult time relating to and communicating with my family. My parents thought I was a dumb child because I was unable to speak and I could not pronounce words correctly. My speech was unclear because I was unable to communicate effectively.

If I was living in our present environment as a child, I would have been diagnosed with autism, but one thing I do have is a unique type of potential and mental ability. I could sort things out in my head, and I was brilliant and creative with my hands. I was the type of child that grew up with not many friends, playing and doing things alone. I found myself involved in many fights because I could not speak properly to explain or communicate what's on my mind.

Internalizing this diagnosis caused me to become very stubborn and angry. I had low self-esteem because I was unable to read or write. This affected me all the way through high school until I accepted Jesus Christ as Lord and Savior.

With no interest, I didn't care about learning, reading, and writing. Various teachers in school would say I was the black sheep of the family because I was a no-good child that would amount to nothing.

I did not care about anything in the world except my interest in using my hands to do arts and craft, building and breaking stuff. It was a blessing when I got saved. The transformation that took place in my life started immediately.

Because in the past I could not read and write, I was not too fond of school and books. I would have to read a book three or four times just to retain any given subject. My mind wandered a lot with all kinds of thoughts and was unable to stay still, to concentrate, and was troubled with all sorts of ideas and floating imaginations. However, somehow, I was able to pass exams with my logic and mental abilities, to understand what I was reading without being able to read correctly.

So I was able to pass exams, with no distinction or credits but with the average grades.

With this unique ability I possessed, I was able to find employment with great jobs and do smart things. Nobody knew I couldn't read properly because I always kept my distance and tried not to be involved in anything that revealed my inabilities.

My New-Found Faith in God

When I accepted Jesus Christ as Lord and Savior, I got baptized and was filled with the Holy Ghost. My mind illuminated like a lightbulb. I was able to read, understand words and their meanings, able to communicate and speak more fluently, and my ability to reason and debate with others improved significantly. I became more bold and confident as my life became very different from what it was before.

As a child growing up, I remember the devil tried every possible way to kill me. He tried in every possible way. My mother was scared for my life, so she would always be praying for me more than my siblings.

With my new found faith in God, I have this passion for being involved in the church ministries, praying and fasting with friends.

One Saturday morning, I traveled up a mountain to fast and pray. While praying, singing, and reaching out to God, I asked God for wisdom, knowledge and understanding. I wanted to understand, simplify and explain the Word of God to edify myself and others. I did not know at the time that this was a prayer from the bible. This was the prayer King Solomon had prayed to God when he asked for wisdom to govern the people of God.

Something happened that very moment. I am not able to explain with words, but I know I was touched by the hands of God, which transformed my life that very moment, so I had this peace and joy washing all over me.

After I returned from the mountain, I began to experience many visions, dreams, revelations and inspirational words of wisdom. Every night I would see a vision of things I had no prior knowledge and understanding of. I began to understand things not taught to me. I could understand how demonic spirits possess people. I could understand things I had never learned before, and I now understood how demonic spirits were able to possess people.

I saw in a vision how demonic spirits possess their host's body. I was able to understand the Scriptures and developed a love for reading other books. As I continued to read and study on a lot of different topics, my knowledge grew as I understood everything I read. It seemed like I understood what I was reading before I even read it, thus confirming what was already in my spirit.

I was developing unique ways I could not understand. The Lord was leading me to the deliverance ministry.

My parents have attended the Redemption Church of God for nearly sixty years and every year, the church holds their yearly convention. At the beginning of my new found spiritual journey, I attended one of the yearly conventions and I met a bishop, now Apostle Bethel, who was preaching and ministering at the convention. A voice spoke to me in my spirit, "Stay very close to that man, he has something to do with you shortly."

I would always be in touch and developed a good relationship with him. The Spirit of the Lord did not give me the reason why I should get close to him.

For many years, I followed him, called him and kept in touch with him. I received good advice from him as my spiritual faith grew, and Apostle Bethel was the one who ordained me as a pastor. We stopped communicating shortly thereafter and I didn't understand or know why.

John the Baptist came into my spirit. His only purpose was to baptize Jesus. Apostle Bethel's purpose was to ordain me as a pastor. He is a good and honorable man of God.

Shortly after I was ordained as a pastor, I started a church ministry. However, it did not last for long. It was not what God wanted for me at that time. God said in my spirit, *The purpose for you starting a church was to be ordained and anoint you as a pastor, to operate in the Spirit with the anointing of a priest.*

A new assignment was given to me by God. I was anointed by God, with the anointing oil poured upon me and my wife by an anointed apostle of God, who ordained me as a pastor to serve at the highest level of the anointing to accomplish God's purpose for ministry. I now understand how important this is. To serve, to operate and to pray in the Spirit of God, I had to have the anointing of a pastor in order to operate with all the gifts of the Spirit. As a pastor, I can provide prayers, counseling, and guidance to the people of faith who have so many different concerns and complicated problems.

The Prayer-Line Ministry

The spirit of the Lord instructed me to start a prayer line in 2008, shortly after the church stopped. It seems, according to how I felt in my spirit, I had no choice but to keep and maintain the prayer line no matter what it takes.

When I first started, I had no support. It seems though, it was a requirement and the thing to do to take me where God wanted me to go. I felt foolish at first, and everything made no sense to me.

I was a newly ordained pastor, with no church or congregation on a prayer line with no members or support, just got laid off from my job with lots of bills and responsibility. Many times, I felt discouraged with deep pain of sorrow in my heart, but I had this determination to stay consistent.

However, experience is an excellent teacher, and in writing this book, the ten years of isolation taught me and trained me well in the school of the Holy Spirit with zeal and determination to do the work of God.

I was very consistent with the prayer line, choosing not to give up, or perhaps, I had no say in the matter. For the past ten years of discipline, I am humbled with the responsibility God has blessed me with. Having the prayer line, three nights per week every week for over ten years is a blessing from God. It didn't matter if it was sunshine, rain, or a hurricane outside, I kept the prayer line going with occasional help from my wife Michelle and prophetess Charmaine. When God anoints you to a position of authority and responsibility, you must be consistent and strong even when faced with adversary.

I could not stop. There were times when it was just me on the prayer line with no support. God requires me to do the prayer line every day in the month of December for the past ten years without a break. I stay online for an hour of prayer and ministry. If I am the only one online, I still pray and minister as if I'm speaking to a congregation or the angels of the Lord.

Then I started to understand what Isaiah 49 was saying, that he concealed me from everyone, and had me in the corner of my room, praying all the time to guide and counsel people.

Something unusual happened during hurricane Irma in September 2017. Internet and phone services were disrupted during the hurricane; however, I was still able to make calls and be on the prayer line in the corner space in my room. God will keep you safe and see you through the fiercest storms. Praise the Lord.

I'm not overly righteous. I am a person who lives to learn to love the Lord and practice obedience, not something that I want to do but something I must do.

Visions from the Lord

I wanted to go to a theological college for leadership training with the advice from my bishop. After consulting with my bishop, I had a dream that week I was in a classroom with other students, and they were all dressed inappropriately to be trained as leaders of the church. It is not the type of look God desires in the people He chooses to represent Him as leaders in the church.

I heard in my spirit, *This is not for you. I will teach you Myself in the school of the Holy Spirit.*

A lot of my teaching and understanding is direct from the Holy Spirit. I am motivated and inspired by the Word of God. David said he encouraged himself in the Lord. I live by those words.

Praise the Lord for the things that I now know and have come to understand. God has taken me on a journey completely different from the traditional church training and practices. Because this was a different learning process, I had to rely on the voice of God during this journey. I have learned everything just by listening to His voice.

I understand some things that don't make sense to other people.

Once I asked the Lord to show me what we would like after the rapture.

One day at four in the morning, I heard a voice said, *Come!* I found myself in the atmosphere, clothed in a bright white garment. My eyes could see clearly, and everything was made known to me. There is no questions with God in heaven, only answers.

I was able to know things without being told. The garment I wore resembled a priest's robe but it was different. It covered my entire body except my head, hands and feet. This garment could not be soiled, could not be removed from my body. When I touched it, it felt like my skin. My body was like a priestly robe—could not be wrinkled, stained, removed.

I was able to understand that this garment was my body. My body radiated the glory of God because His presence covered me. This garment was not a personal garment, but the glory of God is the garment that includes me. According to the Spirit of counsel, it is the garment prepared for the saints of God for the rapture.

Chapter 2

The Third-Dimensional Man

Lukewarm Christians

God is incredible and amazing. We live in a time when not many people understand what life is all about. They are living a life with no spiritual awareness, void of wisdom and understanding that would enable them to have the very basic common sense.

Day after day, people are living a life of hopelessness, lack of knowledge to make wise judgment, having no control over their own actions. Some form of influence beyond them is shaping their future and destiny, which has impacted their lives to look to something or someone for help, to understand how to cope with the stress and frustrations of life. However, those to whom you're seeking guidance and answers themselves need guidance.

There are so many lukewarm Christians who are living their lives and have no knowledge of the truth concerning the Word of God. They are motivated and entertained by the world. The evil that exists has total influence and control over their actions, behavior, and decisions. They know not that they have unlimited power in the Lord Jesus Christ, the source for our strength.

For us to understand our pain and suffering, we must look at where it all began.

Where It All Began

In the beginning, God created the heaven and the earth, and the surface of the earth was without form and void, and darkness was upon the face of the deep.

In Genesis 1:1, you have a perfect world; and in Genesis 1:2, a world filled with chaos. The more we understand what took place in our beginnings, the easier our problems are resolved. We know for sure that there was this angel by the name Lucifer, created by God to be perfect and uniquely designed. He was not an ordinary angel; he was the anointed cherubim, a winged angel, and a protector. He was in the presence of God and became attracted to the attributes of God. What seemed reasonable and attractive to him became terrible and destructive.

He was never created to have independence and express emotions, and his heart corrupted him, and pride became evident in him. God cast him from His presence in the kingdom of heaven and the entire kingdom on earth, and a third of the angelic host fell with him, and led to the destruction of all living creatures.

Darkness Established

The Bible says that darkness was upon the face of the deep. This darkness was when Lucifer became the serpent in his fallen state, absent from the light of God's presence. Likewise, when man disobeyed God to eat of the tree in the garden, the privileges and relationship he had talking with God in the cool of the morning, his supernatural ability, and godly wisdom to name all the animals ended the day God cast him out of the garden.

Likewise, Lucifer was stripped from his title and position with God in heaven. When he was cast out, the light in him became darkness, which created a newly established kingdom: the kingdom of darkness.

We know that Jesus Christ is the light of the world. Prior to when light was spoken into existence, the sun, moon, and the stars were not yet created. God then divided the Light from the Darkness.

> Moreover, the light shineth in darkness; and the darkness comprehended it not. (John 1:5)

The powers and authorities in the heavenly places represent the fallen angels bound in chains, which is symbolic to the embodiment of darkness, and concealed from the light of God.

The chaotic earth was their dwelling place. The earth is the center of the universe and from the first earth, God created all the planets.

The earth was without form and void, and darkness was upon the face of the deep. The Spirit of God moved upon the face of the waters. The Bible says "without form and void." Could this be interpreted that the earth was in a lawless state and everything was in chaos? Also, *void* means "no natural life or activities."

Rebuilding and Restoration

God came to restore and reestablish order and had a plan in mind to reform, rebuild and replenish the earth that was in a chaotic state. He perfected the earth and formed the universe and divided the first earth to create our present solar system. The plan of God went into effect by the spoken Word: "Let there be."

The Spirit of God moved upon the face of the waters. God said, "Let there be a firmament in the midst of the waters, and let it divide the waters from the waters."

God made the firmament and divided the waters which were under the firmament from the waters which were above the firmament, and it was so. God called the firmament heaven; the evening and the morning was the second day (Genesis 1:2, 6–8).

To my understanding, the first earth was entirely different from the second reformed earth.

Earth before was covered with water. We know water can be in three states: solid, liquid, and vapor. God said, "Let there be a firmament in the midst of the waters, and let it divide the waters from the waters." The water was in the state of vapor, and God divided the vapor. He divided the firmament in two; the upper and lower. The upper, He called the heavens. There, He created the planets, the sun, the moon, and the stars. The lower formed the earth and the sea.

The earth is at the center of the universe, and Adam was given dominion over the entire world, all the planets including the earth, the sun, the moon, and the stars. Satan inherited all this real estate due to the fall of man.

Satan established the kingdom of darkness where he now holds fallen man captive in chains of bondage, separated from God. He also promised Jesus Christ he would give the world to him if only He bowed down and worshiped him.

> Also, the devil, taking him up into a high mountain, shewed unto him all the kingdoms of the world in a moment of time. And the devil said unto him, all this power will I give thee, and the glory of them: for that, was delivered unto me; and to whomsoever, I will I give it. If thou, therefore, wilt worship me, all shall be thine. (Luke 4:5–7)

The kingdoms of the world shown to Jesus Christ in a moment are the three domains of this world, consisting of the heavens, earth, and sea. The heavens consist of all the planets, the sun, moon, and the stars. The earth's geological landscape consists of all countries and islands. The sea or ocean is known to be the kingdom of the underworld. Satan knew what he was talking about and has a clear understanding of the power he now possesses through the fall of Adam.

God's Newly Established Kingdom

God, in His wisdom, established the new kingdom in Himself: the body of Jesus Christ, the church of the Living God. Man, by choice, will be able to escape the kingdom of darkness through Christ by faith, which is the door for salvation, eternal life, and happiness.

Thy kingdom come, thy will be done on earth as it is in heaven. The power of God made manifested and known to man by the church through the Gospel of Jesus Christ, in His death, burial, resurrection, and ascension, and the outpouring of the Holy Spirit.

> For God so loved the world, that he gave his only begotten Son, that whosoever believeth in him should not perish, but have everlasting life. For God sent not his Son into the world to condemn the world; that the world through Him delivered. (John 3:16--17

We would think, the problem of the world all started due to Adam's disobedience to God when he ate of the fruit from the tree. I grew up believing that story but thanks be to God for His word and the revelation of the Holy Spirit, God revealed a mystery to me. The fall of man was part of the mystery of God to give birth to the kingdom of heaven on earth to overthrow Satan's kingdom through the broken body of Jesus Christ.

Thy kingdom come, thy will be done on earth as it is in heaven. God planned to allow Satan to take control over Adam's dominion—over the birds of the air, fishes of the sea, beasts of the field—so Jesus Christ could come in the body of a fallen man to overthrow the prince of darkness.

> Moreover, the devil said unto him, all this power will I give thee, and the glory of them: for that delivered unto me; and to whomsoever, I will I give it. (Luke 4:6)

For this has been the plan of God that went into effect when God the Father sent His Son into the world. The primary purpose was to destroy the works of the devil, and in so doing, man will be saved.

So this was the plan of God. The Father sent His Son and said, "Son, we have a situation here. This angel that we created perfect, something has gone wrong. Darkness is in him. I need for you to go and fix what went wrong."

There was only one thing God knew not, and that was sin and the complexity of darkness. He could not identify Himself with the man and what he has become.

> For the Father hath made Jesus his Son to be
> sin for us, who knew no sin; that we might
> be made the righteousness of God in him.
> (2 Corinthians 5:21)

For the plan of God to happen, Jesus Christ the Son of God would enter this world and defeat Satan, and the Earth would be reformed even better than what it was before. Jesus chose to manifest His presence here on earth in the image and likeness of man. He would become sin, and allow Satan to believe he had victory over man in his fallen state. Jesus would overthrow Satan by becoming a sacrificial offering for man's sin through his death, burial and resurrection.

God created man in His image and after His likeness. It was the image and likeness of Himself for His earthly manifestation in the body of Jesus Christ.

The man was essential to God because the Father loves His Son.

We become joint heirs with Him by faith. The Father sees the Son, and the Son recognizes us, for we are His people.

After God created all the living creatures, the birds, beasts, and fishes, He stooped down and formed man from the earth and breathed into his nostrils the breath of life, and man became a living soul.

This was the type of body the Son of God received while on His mission to destroy the works of darkness and Lucifer, the fallen one.

Jesus Christ had to have a body. He is the Word of God, the Creator of all things. He appeared on earth in various ways. He also revealed Himself as the Angel of the Lord.

But angels have limitations. They are unable to express emotions and interact within the natural world because they are spiritual beings. One such appearance Jesus Christ made in the old testament in the manifestation of the Angel of the Lord was with Shadrach, Meshach, and Abednego in the fiery furnace.

> He answered and said, Lo, I see four men loose walking in the midst of the fire, and they have no hurt; and the form of the fourth is like the Son of God. (Daniel 3:25)

Because Jesus needed a physical body for His appearance on earth, He had to be born through a woman, a virgin, so that the sins of Adam would not be in Him, in order to fulfill the mystery of God

> For sin by man came death, by man also came the resurrection of the dead. For as in Adam all die, even so in Christ shall all be made alive. (1 Corinthians 15:21–22)

The Father knew not sin but the fall of Lucifer brought about sin and utter desolation and destruction. For God to destroy the works of darkness, He had to become what Lucifer had experienced; and that was sin. He crafted the body of a man, and He put His Son in a physical body. God was careful when doing this because He did not want His Son, Jesus Christ to inherit the sins of Adam, but would instead inherit the seed of the Holy Spirit.

When Jesus Christ died, He had no sin, and it caused a breach in the realm of the spirit. The Bible says that the wages of sin are death. Jesus Christ had no sin, so He never should have experienced death. That was the plan of God from the beginning, but the devil knew not. Satan, in his pride, thought to himself that when the Son of Man died, he would gain victory and power, ascend above the heavens, and be like God. However, there was no sin found in Christ. When the Spirit of the Lord descended into the belly of the earth, darkness covered the face of the earth to celebrate its victory over the Son of Man. But suddenly, there was a mighty rumbling, a shaking of the earth like a powerful earthquake.

Jesus Christ is the Creator of heaven and earth. He is the one and true living God, the Light of the world, a righteous man without sin and He was put to death. Because He never should have experienced death because He had no sin, chaos ensued, and there was a shaking at the core of the realm of darkness.

Like a nuclear explosion, the gates of the underworld were destroyed. All the righteous people of God who were held captive, beginning with Adam to the thief on the cross to whom Jesus Christ spoke "you shall be with me in paradise" were released from their imprisonment.

The Holy Spirit of God raised Christ from the dead, along with all the righteous men held captive for four thousand years. Paradise was known to exist in the underworld where the righteous souls were held captive until they were freed by the resurrection of Christ. Paradise was mentioned by Jesus in Luke 16:19–31 when He told the story of Lazarus, how he died, and then was carried by the angels to the bosom of Father Abraham.

Paradise was completely destroyed by the power of the resurrection. Praise the Lord!

Jesus, when He had cried again with a loud voice, yielded up the ghost. Moreover, "behold, the veil of the temple was rent in twain from top to bottom, and the earth did quake, and the rocks rent. And the graves opened, and many bodies of the saints which slept arose" (Matthew 27:50–52).

When Jesus Christ came to life, death, hell, and the grave were overthrown because there was a breach in the realm of the spirit and in the underworld. God did not destroy the devil when he fell, but what He did was to establish a plan to confront and defeat Satan at his games. This is the power of the church today: the death, burial, resurrection, and ascension of the Lord Jesus Christ.

It was necessary for Adam to fall so that the Son of Man would inherit the sins of Adam, be crucified, and raised from the dead. Death would not be able to restrain Him because He had no crimes. That was the mystery of God to be unveiled to destroy the works of darkness.

For as in Adam, all died, so in Christ shall all be made alive.

There was a reason for the fall of Adam. It was very strategic and necessary. Before he eats of the tree, the Lord said to him, "Don't touch the fruit of the tree. The day when you eat of it, you shall surely die."

When the law was given to the man, he died. The Word of God says, "Before the law, there was no sin, but when the law, was given, sin sprang to life, and I died." Sin sprang to life in Adam before he ate of the tree, and after Adam fell, there was a redemption plan in place.

One day for God is like a thousand years for man. Man has been living on earth for thousands of years, experiencing all kinds of tribulations, troubles, and trials. The man had to go through a process to be humbled, broken, and willingly surrender his independence from God and become dependent on God. This process was designed to refine man so he could learn to trust in God, and desire the will of God over his own self-will.

In the process, man will become what God wants him to be, not a perfect creation, but much more by desiring and striving toward perfection. God is perfect, and He wants man to be perfect but man must be the one who strives for perfection by desiring the will of God. This is the new order that was established. But every man in his own order: Christ to first fruits; afterward they that are Christ's at his coming. (1 Corinthians 15:23) Christ is the first-fruit, the firstborn from the dead, and everyone who comes after Him will inherit His life. Christ has set a stage for mankind that we can receive life eternal through Christ. We were that model for God, for Christ to use our body and our likeness to destroy the kingdom of darkness.

Then cometh the end, when He shall have delivered up the kingdom to God, even the Father; when he shall have put down all rule and all authority and power. For he must reign, till he hath put all enemies under his feet. The last enemy that shall be destroyed is death (1 Corinthians 15:24–26).

The death that we are experiencing today is due to sin. Satan has no power. He uses the fear of death as a weapon against man to keep him hostage and to accept defeat. Because of a lack of knowledge, the people of God perish.

Jesus Christ, the Son of God, adopted our sinful state to deliver the kingdom of darkness to His Father and, in the process, was transformed into a superhuman God, the Third-Dimensional Man, Christ, the anointed one.

The first-dimensional man, Adam, in his fallen state when he ate of the tree, was cast from the presence of God. The people in the world today are living in sin because they are in total separation from God. They are under the control of evil spirits when fulfilling the nature of the flesh and are therefore in full rebellion against God.

The second-dimensional man are the born-again believers redeemed by the blood of Jesus Christ through faith. By accepting Him as Lord and Savior, and being baptized and filled with the Holy Spirit, they walk by faith, not by sight. They walk not desiring the lust of the flesh but the leading of the Holy Spirit.

The Third-Dimensional Man is Jesus Christ in His risen state, bone and flesh, with no blood. He is like the angels, but far more superior. He can exist in the spiritual and natural world simultaneously with His new superhuman body without having to manifest a body for either world. In the natural world, He can eat and fellowship with man, have a distinct personality and express emotions. The saints of God will be transformed and be just like Christ during the rapture. This is the final mystery to be accomplished and unveiled.

> Behold, I shew you a mystery; We shall not all sleep, but we shall all be changed, in a moment, in the twinkling of an eye, at the last trump: for the trumpet shall sound, and the dead shall be raised incorruptible, and we shall change. For this corruptible must put on incorruption, and this

mortal must put on immortality. (1 Corinthians 15:51–53, KJV)

So also is the resurrection of the dead. It is sown in corruption, it is raised in incorruption. Sown in dishonor, raised in glory. Sown in weakness, raised in power. Sown a natural body, it is raised a spiritual body. There is a physical body, and there is a spiritual body. Moreover, so it is written. The first man Adam was made a living soul, the last Adam created a quickening spirit.

Howbeit that was not first which is spiritual, but that which is natural; and afterward that which is spiritual. The first man is of the earth, earthy man, the second man is the Lord from heaven. As is earthy, such are they also that are earthy: and as is heavenly, such are they also that are heavenly. So, as we have borne the image of the earthy, we shall also bear the image of the heavenly. (1 Corinthians 15:42–49)

Chapter 3

The Fall of Lucifer

The Required Understanding

There is a war taking place in the realm of the spirit, and if we don't understand how to fight spiritual warfare, to push back against these unseen forces and powers coming against us, we will indeed be defeated.

> My people destroyed for lack of knowledge: because thou hast rejected instruction. (Hosea 4:6)

Many good people who love the Lord and desire God's provisions and protection are perishing and they do not know or understand the reasons for their pains, struggles, and sufferings.

It's very simple. If you want to bake a cake, you need to know the recipe, have the correct ingredients, and know the correct temperature to bake the cake. You also have to know how long to bake it. Without any of the above, you can't even get started. You need knowledge and understanding of how to bake a cake if you want to become a good baker. The more knowledgeable you become as a baker, the more experienced and efficient you will be at baking any type of cake and achieving excellent results. It's the same thing with our faith. The more you know and understand the Word of God, the more confidence you will have in Him. The more you know and understand the Word of God, the more comfortable you will be in Him to obtain the desired results to make you stronger and much wiser.

Lucifer, the Chief of All Angels

Lucifer, before the fall, was a special angel in heaven. There was no other angel like him. He had a unique appearance and he held a unique position in heaven which kept him in the presence of God always. There were no other angels like him. He held a unique position in heaven and had a unique appearance in heaven. Sometimes people who have unique gifts and calling don't amount to anything. They die young. They don't live a full life to realize their full potential and become a role model and become the story of legend. Something always seems to go wrong. My observation with them is that these people who have unique callings and abilities will do great things and influence many people.

Lucifer, the chief of all angels, held the highest position in heaven. But he was demoted, stripped of all his titles, and cast out of heaven. He became the chief architect in this crumbling world since the fall of Adam. This great angel was brought down to nothing.

> Thou hast been in Eden the garden of God; every
> precious stone was thy covering. (Ezekiel 28:13)

In Genesis 2:15, it reads, "And the LORD God took the man and put him into the garden of Eden to dress it and to keep it." We know Eden is the garden of God because the garden was mentioned when Adam was first placed there and also during the interaction between Eve and the serpent. There was nothing mentioned about a Lucifer in Eden, the garden of God, in Genesis. That means this will take us back to the first earth.

In Genesis chapter 1:1–2, it reads, "In the beginning, God created heaven and the earth, and; the Earth was without form and void, and darkness was upon the face of the deep." There was something that happened between verse 1 and 2. For reference, the scripture mentions in Ezekiel 28:13 the garden of God in Eden. It also mentions Lucifer before the fall and after the fall, when he was renamed the dragon, that old serpent also known as the devil and Satan (Revelation 20:2).

Lucifer was a unique creation of God, and he was placed in the garden of God. The Word of God described him in the following way: every precious stone was his covering, the Sardis, topaz, diamond, beryl, onyx, jasper, sapphire, emerald, carbuncle, and gold.

> The quality of thy tablets and thy pipes; was prepared in him in the day that thou, was created.

Lucifer was in the garden of God. Within this uniquely created angel were all the precious stones and musical instruments. The Bible says there was praise and worship, hymns and songs in him. Also, in understanding what the Spirit of the Lord was saying to me, Lucifer was placed in the Garden of Eden in the presence of God to be a protector of the glory and presence of God because that was the desired job for the cherubim.

The cherubim were the angels that were placed upon the ark of the covenant with two wings touching each other. They were also stationed at the gate of Eden with swords set in all direction to protect the tree of life, and to guard against the man Adam, should he touch or eat of the tree and live forever in his fallen state.

> So, he drove out the man; and he placed at the east of the garden of Eden Cherubim's, and a flaming sword which turned every direction, to keep the way of the tree of life. (Genesis 3:24)

So Lucifer was a cherubim, a winged angel, a protector of the presence of God, beautiful to behold with musical hymns and worship songs, uniquely designed to the glory of God. We now know that the cherubim are the protectors of the glory of God; and to my understanding, according to the Spirit of Counsel, when the presence and glory of God radiated from the throne of God, the brilliance and radiance of God would reflect from Lucifer to brighten up the heavens, and the angels would see the beauty of God's glory radiating from Lucifer. This made Lucifer special amongst the angels as he was the only one who held this important position so close to God.

> Thou art the anointed cherub that covered; and I have set thee so: thou were upon the holy moun-

tain of God; thou hast walked up and down in
the midst of the stones of fire. (Ezekiel 28:14)

The stone of fire was the manifested state of the *Son* of God,
also known as the *Word* of God, who is Jesus the Christ, our Savior
and Lord today, Hallelujah!

Though was perfect in thy ways, from the day
that thou, was created till iniquity found in thee.
(Ezekiel 28:15)

So to our knowledge of the Bible, we only read in Genesis 2:5
that Adam was placed in the garden of God to take care of it, and
there was also a serpent in the garden. Moreover, the serpent tempted
the woman to take a fruit from the forbidden tree, and she gave to
the man the fruit to eat, and he did eat, and their eyes were both
opened. They both fell from God's grace.

There was nothing mentioned about this angel, this anointed
cherub, that he was in the garden of God. The protector was able
to move freely upon the mountain of God. Could this mountain
be Mount Sinai mentioned in Scripture? This is something to think
about. Also, could this place have existed before the new earth was
reformed?

However, something happened that changed everything! When
Lucifer was in the garden of God, the Bible says that he was created
perfect in all his ways, from the day he was formed until iniquity was
found in him. If he was created perfect, how could iniquity be found
in him?

By the multitude of thy merchandise, they have
filled the midst of thee with violence, and thou
hast sinned: therefore, I will cast thee as profane
out of the mountain of God: and I will destroy
thee, O covering cherub, from the midst of the
stones of fire. (Ezekiel 28:16)

What did God mean when He said "I will destroy thee?" Satan is still roaming the earth creating many problems today. Could God have meant He was going to destroy the power, authority and title Lucifer held on the first earth before the first earth was totally destroyed?

> In the Beginning, God created the heaven and
> the earth. (Genesis 1:1)

Now the serpent was more crafty (subtle, skilled in deceit) than any living creature of the field which the Lord God had made. Who was this serpent in the garden of God? Also, how did he appear? I was able to understand this through the Spirit of Counsel. The serpent is the name given to Lucifer in his fallen state: after he was cursed by God after the fall of man. He is also known as Satan, the devil and other names throughout the ages but it is the same individual, same personality.

Lucifer means "bearer of light, morning star, splendor." The serpent was not a snake before the fall of Adam; this was the name given to him by God describing his present fallen state, in the absence from the position and place with God. However, he was still a winged angel in the garden of God, when he appeared to the woman with the now given name serpent meaning subtle, skilled, and very deceitful, more so than all the creatures in the field and man whom the Lord God had made.

> Thine heart lifted, because of thy beauty, thou
> hast corrupted thy wisdom because of thy bright-
> ness: I will cast thee to the ground, I will lay
> thee before kings, that they may behold thee.
> (Ezekiel 28:17)

Lucifer was always in the presence of God but because pride was found in him, he was cast from heaven, and the entire universe, heaven and the earth was altered between Genesis 1:1 and Genesis 1:2.

And the earth was without form and void and
darkness was upon the face of the deep.

The earth was in isolation, desolation, and frozen for billions
of years. Then the Spirit of the Lord moved upon the face of the
waters. The rebuilding, re-molding and reshaping process began
with the spoken *Word* of God to reestablish the earth once more for
habitation.

What caused Lucifer, the chief of all angels, uniquely designed
and created by God, to fall?

How art thou have fallen from heaven, O Lucifer,
son of the morning! How art thou cut down to
the ground, which didst weakens the nations!
For thou hast said in thine heart, I will
ascend into heaven; I will exalt my throne above
the stars of God: I will also sit upon the mount of
the congregation, in the sides of the north:
I will ascend above the heights of the clouds;
I will be like the Most High. (Isaiah 14:12–14)

God clearly said that Lucifer spoke from his heart, not from his
mouth. It was in his heart that he sinned. And the Bible says,

Out of the abundance of the heart the mouth
speaks. (Matthew 12:34)

The heart of man is the center of his soul and spirit. If man's
heart is corrupt, it automatically corrupts the man. God sees the
heart of man, not so much the outer appearance. He knows the heart
of man because the heart reveals who you are. You cannot hide anything from the heart. If the heart is corrupt, then man is evil.

David prayed, "Create in me a clean heart and renew the right
spirit within me" (Psalm 51:10).

We must continually clean our heart spiritually because it gets
corrupted.

Lucifer was created beautiful. Worship, beauty, precious stones, music, and everything attractive about God was placed in him when he was created. He was perfect but, how was it that he, that was created perfect became imperfect and defective that he had to be cast out of heaven?

Man, on the other hand, was born in an imperfect world. Man could desire and strive for perfection so that he could receive a change of heart. For Lucifer and the angels that fell with him, there would be no redemption because they were created perfect in the beginning.

> For though had said in thine heart, I will ascend into heaven, I will exalt my throne above the stars of God, I will also sit upon the Mount of the congregation, in the side of the North, I will ascend above the height of the clouds, I will be like the Most High. (Isaiah 14:13–14)

Lucifer, although created perfect and being constantly in the presence of God began to undergo a change in his personality. Something new that was not created in him began to manifest in him.

I understood this by the Spirit of Counsel. When you associate with people, especially if they are people of importance or influence, you begin to adapt their behavior and habits. If you are around people who exhibit immoral behavior, you will develop and embrace such behavior. If you are among people of good practice, you will assume the expression and habits of the more superior or influential personality over you. Here is a wise saying: "Show me your friends, and I will tell you who you are."

Lucifer was in the presence of God continually and began to embrace some of the attributes of God. We know that God is a jealous God who desires praise and worship. Lucifer began to appropriate these very attributes. Because he was not created for such abilities, it corrupted him. He was in the presence of God, so the things of God, the attributes of God, began to affect him. He began to experience and possess something far more than his created abilities. Something else that was not created in him was added to his personality.

He felt like a god and desired praise and worship to himself. Craving all the things that God desires, he wanted all of it for himself. Because he is not God, he could not restrain himself, and his foolish heart corrupted him and destroyed him.

There are things that are good for us that can also be dangerous and destructive to us. For example, if you are sick and given medication, you must take the medication as prescribed, or you will risk overdosing. The thing that was meant for good can now become lethal.

So Lucifer was in the presence of God, and the attributes of God began to attach to him. Like an overdose, it became something other than good. He felt as though he was God and coveted the same things that God desired.

He was discharged from the presence of God, and the entire world and earth was plunged into destruction, chaos, and darkness. Everything stood still.

God had given him a position of authority and power, and when that position became vacant, everything associated with the position ceased to be operational, became irrelevant, and ceased to exist. When a king dies, the kingdom falls unless a new king assumes the title and position. Because Lucifer was the only angel created for that title and position, there was no other angel who could assume the title and position, so when Lucifer fell, the position became vacant and destruction desolation and darkness followed.

Because of the fall, Lucifer lost his position and place in heaven. He had no more light in him, no more glory of God to shine upon him. And what did a light bearer become? Darkness, evil, and everything that is opposite to light, everything that is opposite to right.

What we're experiencing today in this world was triggered by the fall of Lucifer. The kingdom of darkness was now established with Lucifer, now the serpent renamed Satan, becoming the prince of darkness and the god of this dying world.

Now God reestablished the earth, and He created man in His image and His likeness and gave man dominion over everything Lucifer once possessed. God then placed the man in the garden of Eden, the same garden that Lucifer, then known as the serpent, was present in. The man was created perfect, just like Lucifer, but God decided to do something different. Instead of allowing a perfect man to remain in Eden, a paradise created by God, God would allow man to become compromised. Although man was created perfect, God allowed the man to fall so that man could be redeemed, would repent, be re-born, live a perfect life and it would be by man's choice. Man will now choose to become more like God by going through a process of the refinery fire, troubles, trials, tribulations, and persecution rather than to remain in that created perfected state in the image and likeness of God.

We now see today man is facing a lot of troubles, challenges, hardships, and persecutions. Man commits sins by destroying one another continuously over the centuries. Believe it or not, these are the very things that groom us to become more like *God!* Based upon our free will and our choice, when we become more like God, the things that caused Lucifer to fall will not cause us to fall because we would've already gone through the experiences being in a fallen state and open rebellion against God.

Something is compelling in the Word of God. The bad experiences of the past will only help to frame something powerful for our future by faith. Many people dismiss these things as foolish, but the righteous must live by faith! Where we are coming from can only guide us to where we are going. The past will determine your future. You can never ignore past experiences because these are the things that make you; these are the things that will also break you.

You have a spirit in you from God. He will guide and order your steps. Even though you walk through the valley of the shadow of death, fear no evil. The troubles of life are a part of the process. When you have experiences, experiences teach wisdom. Wisdom is application; it's how you apply yourself in your daily challenges of life. If you don't have intelligence, it would be hard for you to make right choices and make good decisions. The Bible says seek wisdom and get knowledge and understanding.

Today we are suffering in this world, and we have no idea how this world is framed. God, in His wisdom and power, revealed to us through His Word how we should live and conduct ourselves. We should study the Word of God and seek and research to have a clear understanding.

So many things are happening, many things that we will never know until told to us for us to have a clear understanding and to build upon it. A seed is good and can stay for centuries and remain a seed. For it to grow, it has to be planted, for the life in the seed must grow in order to break through the shell.

The life of God is within us, and we must die to the flesh—our carnal life, worldly desires, and lustful tendencies—that the life of God will break forth to spiritual empowerment. We will have no desire for God and His righteousness if we don't break out of this shell that imprisons us, that holds us hostage to unforgiveness, lust, greed, and pride. This fleshly manifestation is in open rebellion against the Holy Spirit of God.

With nothing in common with the things about God, we must break ourselves loose from this flesh so that the spiritual man can come alive in us.

Lucifer's pride and selfish desires had nothing in common with God and the things about God, so he was discharged and barred from the light and glory of God.

We must break ourselves loose from this fleshly carnal man that is controlled and governed by Satan, the first fallen, and surrender to Jesus, the first risen, who has transformed us from the kingdom of darkness, Satan's kingdom, to the kingdom of light, that the spiritual man can come alive in us.

We want the presence of God to be in us to shape us and to make us, not to destroy us. We want to be built up by the Spirit of God who will be our guiding light to enable, empower, teach, and frame us and not to break us.

By the example of the fall, there was something found in Lucifer that was never created and placed in him, being in the presence of God and adapting to something that was never meant to be for him. We must learn to appreciate and value who we are personally, how we are created to be, and live our true self in God and strive in His presence to glorify, honor, and praise Him.

Some good things in life not meant for us can turn around to be a thing that will destroy us; therefore, we have to keep on crying out to the Lord to help us, to create in us a clean heart and renew the right spirit in us.

The Bible says we must examine ourselves while we are in the faith and prove ourselves. It is necessary for us to keep an eye on our behaviors, keep an eye on the way we are living, because we can be walking away from God. The things that were meant to deliver, strengthen, and empower can become the very thing that breaks and destroys us. Medication is given for healing purposes, but an overdose will kill you or cause you to lose consciousness of your true self.

In everything that we do, we must do it to the glory of God. We all do things we consider to be right, but if done incorrectly, or the idea or reasons are generated from the wrong source, it will corrupt the heart.

Chapter 4

The Spirit of Darkness

D arkness is a spirit. What causes darkness, and how did darkness come into existence? How was darkness established?

It goes back to Genesis. If you want to know the ending of anything, you must start from the beginning. The Word of God declared, "In the beginning, GOD created the heavens and the earth, and the earth was without form and void, and darkness was upon the face of the deep" (Genesis 1:1–2).

Darkness was upon the face of the deep.

What was this darkness?

In the midst of darkness, God appeared and said, "Let there be *light*," and there was light. God separated the light from darkness, and He called the darkness *night* and called the light *day*.

We have grown up to believe and adopt this principle, that darkness is truly night; but in the realm of the spirit, there is no night, and there's no time.

What is this darkness upon the face of the deep?

If you ask anyone what is darkness, they would say "absence of light," and others will say darkness is blackness, gloominess, dimness, shadow, or shade. They will come with all different types of interpretation. They would say wickedness or evil forces, sin, iniquity, or immorality.

What truly is darkness? I can truly say this by the Spirit of God, the understanding that God has given me concerning this. The Bible talks about Lucifer, how he was created and uniquely built. He was not only an angel; he was a cherub, a winged angel, superior to all other angels that were in heaven. He was a protector of the presence of God; he was a worshiper with all the choruses and hymns in him. He radiated the heavens with radiance and brilliance. The glory of God reflected from him, but then something was found in him that was not supposed to be there, that he was not created with. Pride was found in him. He wanted to ascend above the heavens and be like God. Where did he get that from? When you associate with anything, more likely, over time you begin to adopt the behavior or habits of the person or things you associate with. It's fair to say that Lucifer, being in the presence of God, began to adopt some of the attributes of God. What was good became destructive to him, because he was never created with such abilities, namely the ability to feel or express emotions, such as jealousy and pride.

God is a jealous God, very prideful about his creation. Lucifer began to adopt these attributes, and it corrupted him. The Bible says Lucifer was cast from heaven. Lucifer gave birth to the kingdom of darkness, the first fallen from God's presence. Due to pride and rebellion, he fell from the light, and darkness was established.

Jesus Christ gave birth to a new kingdom on earth, the church due to His death, burial, and resurrection, the first born from the dead.

> Who is the image of the invisible God, the first-born of every creature? (Colossians 1:15)
>
> And he is the head of the body, the church: who is the beginning, the firstborn from the dead; that in all things he might have the preeminence. (Colossians 1:18)
>
> God said I form the light and create darkness, I make peace and create evil. (Isaiah 45:7)

God said he formed light. What does this mean? When you form something, that which it was formed from was from something that already existed. So God formed the light for the purpose to exist in the midst of darkness.

> He bowed the heavens also and came down; and darkness was under his feet. (2 Samuel 22:10)

The Bible says God created darkness. That means darkness was birthed into existence due to the fall of Lucifer because he fell from the *light* of God, the presence of light. Darkness was established. That darkness that was upon the face of the deep represents Lucifer, now Satan, and all those other angels, a third of the angelic host that fell with him.

> For God spared not the angels that sin but cast them down to hell and delivered them into chains of darkness. (1 Peter 2:4)

Chains here is not something physical but darkness itself, the chains meaning that they were bound to evil, bound to wickedness, bound to iniquity, living and existing in everything darkness promotes and represents.

Chains of darkness doesn't mean that they were unable to move around and do nothing. It means that they would never be able to experience God's light or be in the presence of God because darkness becomes the place of operation and dwellings.

> For we wrestle not against flesh and blood, but against principalities, against powers, against the rulers of the darkness of this world, against spiritual wickedness in high places. (Ephesians 6:12)

Principalities, powers, and rulers of this world, working in the atmosphere and the lives of people, circumstances, various situations, and problems are all darkness. When we talk about darkness, we talk about night, but it is not night. It's that evil force that exists and a chain that bounds them there for eternity, awaiting the judgement of God. People are in chains of darkness, but they have a Redeemer, Jesus Christ, to redeem them out of and from darkness.

> For God sent not his Son into the world to condemn the world; but that the world through him might be saved. He that believeth on him

> is not condemned: but he that believeth not is
> condemned already, because he hath not believed
> in the name of the only begotten Son of God.
> And this is the condemnation, that light is
> come into the world, and men loved darkness
> rather than light, because their deeds were evil.
> (John 3:17–19, KJV)

God has established a way of escape for man, the plan for redemption.

> For all have sinned, and come short of the glory
> of God; Being justified freely by his grace through
> the redemption that is in Christ Jesus: Whom
> God hath set forth to be a propitiation through
> faith in his blood, to declare his righteousness for
> the remission of sins that are past, through the
> forbearance of God. (Romans 3:23–25, KJV)
> There is no redemption for the fallen
> angels. We must have a different concept and
> understanding about darkness; night represents
> darkness. But if a man walks in the night, he
> stumbles, because there is no light in him.
> (John 11:10, KJV)

Darkness is evil, the absence of light and the presence of God. It's the devil at work, and that is his domain. When the Lord said, "Let there be light," there appeared the presence of God in the midst of darkness, which represents iniquity, wickedness, dark forces, and the fallen angels.

There was a purpose for God to show up in darkness to overthrow the prince of darkness, who is Lucifer, now Satan, fallen from heaven. Because of the fall, the entire world plunged into utter destruction and was in a frozen state for billions of years. The Son of God appeared in darkness to refurbish, rebuild, and overthrow the prince of darkness and all their works and turn over that kingdom to His *Father*.

> He that committed sin is of the devil; for the devil sinned from the beginning. For this purpose, the Son of God was manifested, that he might destroy the works of the devil. (1 John 3:8)

Jesus Christ came into this world to destroy the prince of darkness. We are redeemed and delivered from the powers of darkness that controlled us. When we start to understand the whole concept, the reason for the coming of Jesus Christ, the reason for His works, what were His intentions, what He desired to accomplish, we will have a totally different understanding and view as to what happened with a totally different perspective. Concerning our faith, we would not take things for granted or mingle and play around with sin.

Sin is destructive. It gives Satan the authority over us. Since he is the first fallen, darkness was created and established, and he became the prince of darkness.

The plan of God was to send His only begotten Son, in the likeness of sinful man. So by allowing man to fall, allowing Satan to gain dominion and total control over man, Jesus Christ, who came in the likeness of sinful man who was under the control of Satan, was able to destroy him from within.

When the devil thought he destroyed the Son of Man by putting him to death on the cross, he was thwarted in his lust to gain power and authority and was defeated, according to Isaiah 14:13–14:

> For thou hast said in thine heart, I will ascend into heaven, I will exalt my throne above the stars of God: I will sit also upon the mount of the congregation, in the sides of the north: I will ascend above the heights of the clouds; I will be like the Most High.

What really happened was, Satan was deceived. He was tricked. There was a law that was established from the beginning: an innocent man without sin could not be put to death.

And God saw the light, that it was good; and God divided the light from the darkness. Jesus Christ is that light.

There was a man sent from God whose name was John. The same came for a witness, to bear witness of the Light, that all men through him might believe. He was not that light but was sent to bear witness of that Light.

That was the true Light, which lighted every man that cometh into the world. He was in the world, and the world was made by him, and the world knew him not.

There is another law that states that the wages of sin is death. Christ had no sin in him. He was never to be put to death, and because that law was violated, a breach occurred in the realm of the spirit of darkness. There was a rumbling, a shaking, a giant earthquake that shook the realm of the spirit of darkness at it's very core. Jesus Christ could not remain dead. By the power of the Holy Spirit, He was raised up from the dead.

The resurrection power of God shook the foundation of hell, death, and darkness. The light of God, Jesus the Christ, the Anointed One, entered into this fallen world through the body of sinful man, and through the foolishness of the cross, Satan was disqualified and overthrown.

Jesus Christ broke darkness from within. How best to destroy something but from within?

Jesus Christ, the Son of the living God, dethroned and overthrew Satan, and the Bible tells you that darkness is under his feet. All principalities, powers, rulers and spiritual wickedness are under the feet of Christ. They are subjected to Him because He has defeated darkness. For this reason, Satan has no power; he is truly powerless.

The only power Satan has is the power of deception to deceive man into surrendering his self-will to him, to gain authority when man rebels against God. Satan gained power through man's rebellion against God. Because Satan is the first fallen, everyone who falls into sin becomes enslaved and subjected to him and falls under his dominion. This is called spiritual slavery.

He's evil and desires to use and control man for his own purpose. But he has no power, so when people continuously rebel against God, walk in sin and disobedience, they are under the control of the demonic forces that work on behalf of the devil. The more you walk upright in truth, the more you will able to walk in the light of God, the more control you have over darkness and evil that leads to sin.

> The Lord said unto Moses stretch out thy hands
> towards heaven, that there may be darkness over
> the land of Egypt, even darkness which may be
> felt. (Exodus 10:21)

When we begin to look at how God has done a mighty work in Exodus 10:21, the darkness could be felt when Moses stretched forth his rod over Egypt. In our life today, we see darkness operating in a way that it can be felt for example sickness, diseases, famine, plague, violence, and destruction.

This is not darkness as we think of night, but a more oppressive and evil force. When darkness appears, it brings about emptiness, sufferings, pain, death and poverty. It brings about all types of evil that would be the working of Satan, the chief of darkness. He's able to manipulate man because man is in a fallen state.

He had no claim to Jesus Christ because there was no sin in Him. He was perfect in every way. What defeated Satan was when he allowed the Son of Man to be crucified. Because there was no sin in Christ, the resurrection power gave birth to the kingdom of God. The church of the living God was birthed, so we are no ordinary people. We are extraordinary people birthed into the kingdom of God.

> The word is nigh thee, even in thy mouth, and
> in thy heart: that is, the word of faith, which we
> preach; That if thou shalt confess with thy mouth
> the Lord Jesus, and shalt believe in thine heart
> that God hath raised him from the dead, thou

shalt be saved. For with the heart man believeth
unto righteousness; and with the mouth confession is made unto salvation. (Roman 10:8–10)

If we continue to live and abide by the teachings in the Old
Testament, we will fail spiritually. We must adopt and live by the
principal and teachings of the New Testament of Jesus Christ, which
is the Gospel. The Gospel of Jesus Christ, when the outpouring of
the Holy Ghost is given, the Spirit of God that lives within us regen-
erates our spirit. If anyone has not the Spirit of God, they are none
of His.

When you hear the word, believe in your heart and confess
from your mouth that Jesus Christ is the Son of the living God.
You are now a new creation in Christ. The Spirit of God transforms
your spirit to become a son of God, adopted into the kingdom that
is being birthed through the resurrection of Jesus Christ. When the
people of God adopt beliefs and religious doctrines that are not fully
aligned with the true teachings and preaching of the gospel of the
kingdom of our Lord and Savior Jesus Christ, our faith becomes
powerless and weak.

No one in the Old Testament could cast out a demon. The
devil was never mentioned in the Old Testament except for three
times. The reason why is because he had power. He was the prince
of darkness.

Jesus Christ was able to challenge the devil because He had no
sin in Him. He could cast out demons. We today have the power
through Christ to cast out demons, heal the sick, give sight to the
blind, and work miracles. Jesus Christ gained that victory through
the cross. Believers should never allow darkness to control them. We
must control darkness because we have power through Christ. We
are seated with Christ in the heavenly places, seated in the light of
God.

So we must take control over everything because God has given
us the authority to do so. That's why we must never be afraid to use
the name of Jesus Christ. We must declare Him for who He is. He is
the Author and Finisher of our faith. Our rock and shield and hiding

place, the one and true Eternal God who has given us the authority over darkness because we are called into the presence of Light.

So whenever a Christian believer surrenders themselves to sin, they surrender themselves to the prince of darkness to be in control over their lives. It is necessary for believers to be consistent in their faith in the Lord Jesus Christ.

Chapter 5

The Fall of Man Was Necessary

There are many things that we need to know, things that we shouldn't take for granted. The Bible says, "My people are destroyed for lack of knowledge because thou has rejected knowledge" (Hosea 4:6). There are times when information is critical for the development of our faith, deliverance, and transformation. Believers tend not to want to know, choose not to know, block their minds, suppress their feelings or don't want to find out because it doesn't go in line with the things they believe in because facing that truth can be very painful.

> Study to show thyself approved unto God, a workman that needed not to be ashamed, rightly dividing the word of truth. (2 Timothy 2:15)

It is imperative to have knowledge and understanding about the Word of God to pray effectively. When dealing with the stronghold that causes uncontrollable behavior that influences your life, and not being able to call it by name or identify the source for the cause, it will not listen or respond. That stronghold will behave as if you're not talking to it, if not addressed or called by name.

It's essential to know and have a clear understanding dealing with these types of circumstances. It is also important not to be easily dismissive or disagreeable to things you don't know or understand without verifying for truth.

In the previous chapter, we were talking about the fall of Lucifer, how Lucifer was created most beautiful amongst all the angels. He was uniquely built, designed and equipped with "things that no other angel has or possesses." There was something else found in him that was not a part of or should be associated with his design or makeup.

Pride was found in his heart, so it corrupted him. The angels were created perfect; they are spiritual beings. Not designed with a heart, they cannot express emotions and self-will. However, there was something found in Lucifer that was not a part of his design, and he started to behave differently, which caused him to fall from the light, the presence of God. *Lucifer* means "light bearer," and he became the serpent by name. After the fall, darkness was established.

Lucifer was named the serpent, then *Satan* after God cursed him in the Garden of Eden when he deceived the man and his wife. He became the prince of darkness when he inherited Adam's authority. Now defeated in the death, burial, and resurrection of Jesus Christ, the Son of God, Satan is now seeking after whom he may devour.

> God created man in His image, in the Image of
> God created He them; male and female created
> them. (Genesis 1:27)

Man's spirit, created in the image of God, likened unto Father, Son, Holy Spirit, three personalities one God, male and female, two personalities, one spirit, named man. The Word of God makes it clear: God is not a man in fleshly form (Numbers 23:19); God is a Spirit (John 4:24).

On the seventh day, God rested (Genesis 2:12). After God rested on the seventh day, He formed a physical body for man out of the dust of the ground, and breathed into his nostrils the breath of life, and man became a living soul (Genesis 2:7).

God formed a body for the spiritual man; the male and female spirit he created was one; in the image and likeness of God. Then God called the man that he had formed Adam; meaning red dirt. There was no help mate suitable for Adam. God then form a body for the female from the Rib of Adam and Adam called the female now in her own body Woman.

And Adam said this is now the bone of my bone and flesh of my flesh: she shall be called Woman, because she was taken out of man (Genesis 2:23).

The man became a living soul, self-conscious, world-conscious, God-conscious, with an active mind, self-will, emotion, passion, and desires, with the ability to interact with nature and the spiritual. So it is fair to say that man was created as a spirit, male and female, in the same spirit, image, and likeness of God.

Also, God blessed them, and God said unto them, "Be fruitful and multiply and replenish the earth and subdue it and have dominion over the fish of the seas, the fowls of the air, and over every living thing that moves upon the earth." God gave the man this charge to replenish, restore, repair, restock, and refill the whole earth because every living thing on the first earth was destroyed because of the fall of Lucifer.

God also had something in mind when He gave man dominion, power, and authority—the same dominion and power Lucifer had before the fall. However, God chose to go further because the man spirit would not be able to manifest in a physical form, so God decided to give the man a physical body to live in so that he would be able to adapt to live in the natural world.

Angels are spiritual beings able to manifest in a physical state, but their manifested image comes with limitations. The physical body is uniquely designed for the Son of God's manifestation into the world for destroying the works of the devil (1 John 3:8). So this body was not formed for eternal existence but for the temporal purpose.

> For we know that if our earthly house of this tabernacle were to dissolve, we have a building of God, a house not made with hands eternal in the heavens. (2 Corinthians 15)

So the name Adam given to the man meaning "red soil," meant that man would be able to live and adapt to the newly reformed earth, but the man had limitations in the physical body. For man to reach his full and true potential in God, the fall of man was necessary.

So God planted a garden eastward in Eden, and there He put the man whom he had formed. Eden was a spiritual place but God allowed it to manifest into the natural world so that man, now in a physical form, would be able to live in and tend to the garden. God planted in the midst of the garden the tree of life, and the tree of knowledge of good and evil.

God then put the man in the garden to dress it and keep it, then commanded the man, saying, "Of every tree in the garden you may freely eat, but of the tree of knowledge of good and evil, thou shall not eat, for the day that you eat thereof, you shall surely die." The man was given the name *Adam*.

> Also, the Lord God commanded the man saying, Of every tree of the garden you may freely eat, But the tree of knowledge of good and evil, thou shalt not, eat from it: for in the day that though eat thereof, though shall surely die. (Genesis 2:16–17)

Why would God give the man this commandment?

Adam died the moment the commandment was given unto him not to touch or eat of the tree of knowledge of good and evil, and undoubtedly, he experienced that spiritual death the moment he ate from the tree that was now forbidden by a new law.

> For until the law, sin was in the world, but sin is not imputed when there is no law. (Romans 5:13)
>
> For as by one man's disobedience many were made sinners, so by the obedience of one shall many be made righteous. Moreover, the law entered, that the offense might abound. However, where sin abounded, grace did much more abound: That as sin hath reigned unto death, even so, might grace reign through righteousness unto eternal life by Jesus Christ our Lord. (Roman 5:19–21)

> And out of the ground the Lord God formed every beast of the field and every fowl of the air and brought them unto Adam to see what he would call them, and what so ever Adam called every living creature that was their name there off. (Genesis 2:19)

So Adam had the wisdom to name all the beasts of the field, the fowls of the air, but at the same time, God gave a command not to touch of the tree in the midst of the garden. Why would God not give man the same command by saying, "Thou shall not name all the beasts of the field and the fowls of the air," but only command Adam not to touch the tree?

If Adam had the wisdom to know how to name all the beasts of the field, birds of the air, fishes in the sea, would you also say that Adam should possess the same wisdom to know not to touch or eat of the fruit from the tree in the midst of the garden, the tree of knowledge of good and evil and the tree of life?

> However, sin, taking occasion by the commandment, rots in me all manner of concupiscence. For without the law sin was dead. For I was alive without the law once, but when the commandment came, sin revived, and I died. And the commandment, which ordained to life, I found to be unto death. For sin, taking occasion by the commandment, deceived me, and by it slew me. (Roman 7:8–11)

Now, this is my understanding. The reason why God commanded the man not to eat of the tree was because the fall of man was imminent and necessary, destined to happen. It was essential for man to fall because God wanted man to become far more excellent and superior to whom he was created to be. Jesus Christ represents that manifested excellent state today, in high power and glory through His death, burial, and resurrection.

Now this has to do with man's decision and choice, not whom God created man to be in that Adamic state. But become by choice something far greater and superior to how he was designed to be. Could that have been the reason why God commanded Adam not to eat of the tree of good and evil? However, God did not command the man to name the animals but brought the animals to man to see what Adam would call them.

If Adam had wisdom enough to know how to name all the animals, it's safe to say Adam had intelligence, the God instinct, because he was created in the image and likeness of God, to know not to touch of the tree of life and the tree of knowledge of good and evil.

So when God commanded Adam, "Don't touch!" God established a new law, and in so doing, sin sprang to life.

Without the law, sin was nonexistent. There was no sin that could exist, so now if Adam had eaten of not the tree of life and eaten of the tree of knowledge of good and evil, nothing would have happened. The mere fact that God commanded the man not to eat of the tree created a knowledge of the law which gave birth to sin. Moreover, because of that, the fleshly man sprang to life. Adam will now have the desire for the fruit to eat of it because something sprang to life in Adam when God commanded the man not to eat from the tree.

In our day-to-day life, the more we have laws and commandments, the more we become enslaved and in bondage.

When Jesus Christ died, the veil in the temple, symbolic of the veil of sin that hangs over us, was ripped in the temple, from the top to the bottom. He dismantled all the things that would keep us hostage, keep us in bondage, the laws and commandment, rules and regulation. Don't do this and don't do that.

We are under a new law, the law of the spirit of life in Christ, so we are not under restrictions or bound to do this or to do that, to fulfill the commandment. It's the Spirit of God within you that enables and empowers your will to do through conviction by conscience. Things I used to do, I do them no more. The law of the Spirit of life in Christ will cause you to overcome your sinful desires through temptation.

So when you used to steal and tell lies, because you are now in Christ, you don't want to do it anymore without anyone telling you should not lie and steal. The more you hear, "Don't do this or that," sin takes occasion by those commandment given unto you, and it brings forth death in the flesh. Therefore, sometimes when we feel so controlled and oppressed, so heavy and burdened, it's because we have too much control over us.

The more we are under control, the more oppressed we become. Some people cannot function if they don't have something over them to dictate or keep them in line, and the more you try to get in line by some laws, rules, commandments, and instructions, the more enslaved you become.

We should be directed by the spirit. Trust God for His counsel and wisdom, that we can instinctively know what to do and how to do it. How Adam was created, he understood how to name all the animals, and the Lord said, "It is good." God commanded Adam, "Don't touch of the tree." Adam could instinctively know not to reach of the tree, but the fall of man was necessary.

Adam had to eat of the tree because God had a far much greater plan for man not to remain in the state he was formed with a physical body, but to be transformed in the likeness of Christ Jesus, the Redeemer, our Savior and Lord.

Because when we become like Christ, we shall take on a new frame, new body, and a new life. The life we shall have shall be far more superior than the angels, superior than the created man Adam.

What is a man that thou art mindful of him? The Son of man, that thou visited him? For thou have made him a little lower than the angels and has crowned him with glory and honor, thou made him have dominion over the works of thy hands, thou has put all things under his feet (Psalms 8:4–6).

So the man, created less than angels, then received something more powerful and unique that he excelled far above and beyond the angels. It is essential to know that spiritual man had no limitations because God had created man in His image and after His likeness.

God then put the man in a human body to do work in the garden. This then caused the man to have limitations. God gave man authority over the birds; meaning the atmosphere; the fishes in the sea, the underworld; the beasts of the field and the earth. With the spirit man inside Adam's physical body, he only had authority over the beasts of the field. Adam did not have the ability to operate in the heavens, the terrestrial planets, or into the underworld or the sea. Adam only had the ability to move about the earth.

When God created man in His image, after His likeness, the man was spirit just like the angels, with the ability to go anywhere in the universe. Now in God through Jesus Christ, man will transition or morph into something far more than how he was formed in the flesh. God's plan for man's transformation to come to pass at the appointed time made the fall of man necessary.

> Behold, I shew you a mystery; We shall not all sleep, but we shall all be changed, in a moment, in the twinkling of an eye, at the last trump: for the trumpet shall sound, and the dead shall be raised incorruptible, and we shall change. For this corruptible must put on incorruption, and this mortal must put on immortality. (1 Corinthians 15:51–53)

We are still going through this transitional stage, even right now being redeemed by the blood of the Lamb. That if thou shalt confess with thy mouth the Lord Jesus and shalt believe in thine heart that God hath raised him from the dead, thou shalt be saved. Through our faith in Christ Jesus, we are born into a new kingdom, living a life in Christ Jesus, Christ the firstborn from the dead, the firstborn of all creation.

He came into this world, like one of us and transitioned Himself into a superhuman, far more significant than the angels with no boundaries or limitations. We are bound to earth but there are no boundaries or limitations for Jesus the Christ. He has broken all human barriers because He was sinless. There was no sin found in Him.

God created death, hell, and the grave. The man was enslaved by death because the wages of sin is death. Jesus Christ was birthed into our sinful state and nature, like one of us, but He did not come through the seed of Adam but through the seed of the Holy Spirit.

> He lived a life like an ordinary man, had no sin, never committed sin, for he made himself sin for us, who knew no sin; that we might be made the righteousness of God in him. (2 Corinthians 5:21)

The kingdom of darkness celebrated when they put him to death, but when Jesus Christ died, there was an earthquake, a shaking in the realm of darkness, because He had no sin. He shouldn't have died. He had the gift of God for a sinless life, which is eternal life; but because He died, there was shaking. A breach took place in the kingdom of darkness.

The light appeared in darkness, the mystery of God hidden from the beginning was unveiled. There was a breach, so when He descended to hell, hell could never contain Him because there was no sin found in Him. The wages of sin are death; the gift of God is eternal life.

The Spirit of God raised Jesus Christ from the dead through the resurrection power. He gained strength and authority over death, hell, and the grave. Jesus Christ, through the resurrection power of the Holy Spirit, was transformed into a superhuman—no blood, only bone and flesh. He took on a new life. In the new life He assumed, He had a new body, soul and spiritual man in the image and likeness of God and this new man Christ Jesus is able to exist in the spiritual and natural worlds simultaneously.

The new man Christ Jesus is able to ascend and descend at will to and from heaven, operate in the atmosphere, underworld and in all the different dimensions at the same time. He is not bound by time, by law, or anything because He is now a superhuman man, far superior to the angels standing in the gap for our sins between God and man, the King of kings and the Lord of lords.

Chapter 6

The Serpent's Deception

The Word of God is a lamp to our feet, a light that shines and brightens our pathway. We must accept the Word of God for how it is written, paralleling it with our daily life and in everything we do. There's always something in the Word that coincides with our life experiences.

Paralleling the Word of God with your daily life is a way to know that you are living and operating according to the leading of the Holy Spirit. There must be a correlation in the Word of God concerning everything we do, believe, and observe in the world. Knowing this, you will be able to discern truth from error, and your steps will be ordered and guided with an understanding of the things about God.

> Now the serpent was subtler than any beast of the
> field which the LORD God had made. And he said
> unto the woman, Yea, hath God said, Ye, shall
> not eat of every tree of the garden? (Genesis 3:1)

The Bible refers to the serpent as subtler than all the beasts of the field which the Lord has made. So the serpent was in the garden. It doesn't necessarily mean that the serpent here was a part of the animal kingdom. Now, the serpent was subtler than any other beast of the field which the Lord God has made. What was his purpose? What makes him subtler than all the beasts of the field? Could this be a description of a name and not an individual personality and character described as deceptive, crafty, and cunning?

Why should we think the serpent was a snake? Could we say that Lucifer, the fallen, now Satan, could manifest in the image of a man and appear to Eve in the garden with all the characteristics of being very deceptive, crafty, cunning (meaning "serpent"), as handsome as can be, to cause the woman to be swayed? Nowhere in the Old Testament is it mentioned that the devil was the serpent, but scriptures in the New Testament named the devil as the serpent.

> And the great dragon was cast out, that old serpent, called the Devil, and Satan, which deceived the whole world. (Revelation 12:9)

And he said unto the woman, Yea, hath God said, Ye, shall not eat of every tree of the garden? (Genesis 3:1). So the serpent was able to talk and have a conversation with the woman. We don't know the type of language that was communicated or spoken here. Could it be that the serpent was talking in her mind or vocally speaking from his lips to the woman?

The Bible says that he was communicating with the woman by having a conversation with her. We don't know what the serpent looked like before the curse was pronounced upon him. But we know that the word serpent means deceptive, crafty, and cunning, more so than any other beast in the field.

We also know that there is no place in the Bible that an angel or fallen angel was able to manifest in a beast form. We only know of angels manifesting in human form.

> And the LORD God said unto the Serpent because thou hast done this, thou art cursed above all cattle, and above every beast of the field; upon thy belly shalt thou go, and dust shalt thou eat all the days of thy life. (Genesis 3:14)

God cursed the serpent in the garden to have the character and behavior of a snake. But Satan is not a snake; he is still a fallen angel. He reveals himself as so in Zechariah chapter 3:1 in the Old Testament: "And he shewed me Joshua the high priest standing before the angel of the LORD, and Satan standing at his right hand to resist him." And in the New Testament: "And no marvel; for Satan himself is transformed into an angel of light" (2 Corinthians 11:14).

Now that we know the meaning associated with the serpent, what physical description did the serpent take after God cursed it? Everything that was excellent and good associated with the meaning "serpent" became evil, negative and not to be trusted. The word serpent should never be used as a definite description concerning anything that is good. If someone is called a snake, it brings up the most negative feelings towards that person.

So the serpent was having a conversation with the woman. "Did God say, thou shall not eat of the tree of the garden?" Satan has a way to assert himself in our judgment, to question how much you know and how much you believe. We can know something but not necessarily believe in it. You must have conviction about the things that you know and understand to have positive results.

It's essential that we have conviction concerning the things that we know and understand. If we don't have confidence, our faith will not be at the forefront of spiritual awareness. This will be a problem if there is no conviction, no deep insight, and no spiritual connection with the thing that should build, motivate, and encourage us.

So the woman only knows what she heard, with no wisdom, no knowledge and no understanding of what to do or what not to do. And the serpent said unto the woman, "Yea, hath God said, Ye, shall not eat of every tree of the garden?" And the woman said unto the serpent, "We may eat of the fruit of the trees of the garden, but of the fruit of the tree which is in the midst of the garden, God hath said, Ye shall not eat of it, neither shall ye touch it, lest ye die."

The woman understood what was said, but with no in-depth knowledge guided by wisdom, it is a mistake that can make us vulnerable.

Whenever we hear or see things, don't accept it for what it is without questioning the validity and sincerity, reasons and purposes, behind it; without paying attention to details.

> But of the fruit of the tree which is in the midst
> of the garden, God hath said, ye shall not eat of
> it, neither shall ye touch it, lest ye die.

And the serpent said unto the woman, "Ye shall not surely die" (Genesis 3:3–4). What does this mean? "Not surely die!" There is a big difference between to die and not surely die. The serpent knew that the woman had no idea, what "not surely die" meant. So he was able to twist words to deceive and manipulate the woman's limited knowledge and understanding. By communicating that there was another type of death—"not surely die" the serpent was implying that it was not that bad to disobey God's command. Apparently, if you die in this way, you will be better off and be a better person.

God comes to us with salvation, and said if any man believed in Him and is baptized, he becomes a new creation in Christ. But there is something else associated with our salvation. We must live a holy lifestyle and abstain from sins and any other things or behaviors that can influence us and cause us to become separated from the faith and God.

Satan will attempt to deceive us into believing that we are missing out on all the fun activities everyone else is doing even if we know in our heart it's wrong and goes against God's word. He will try to deceive us into believing that we will be popular with the crowd if we engage in sinful behavior because everyone else is doing it. "You are missing out on all the fun stuff, and you are boring," the devil will say to you. "Why bother to live this dull and boring life in Christ when you could be living it up and having fun?"

So he allows us to see a lot of benefits, a lot of adventures, a lot of attractions that will blow our mind. Oh yes! Our heart bleeds with excitement. We want to be a part of this. It looks good and entertaining; it looks delicious. Desperate anxiety causes us to flaunt ourselves with these things, and not to know it doesn't build us up but break us down.

So the serpent says you shall not surely die, not the kind of death that you are thinking; it is a different kind of death. This death is somewhat much better than the death that you would have experienced. For God knows that in the day you eat thereof, then your eyes shall be open.

So this is a kind of death that the serpent knew God was describing. Your eyes will be open to the truth! This is a different death, not when life seizes to exist in the flesh. For this type of death, your eyes are open when you're able to see things in a different way, independent of your spiritual eyes.

God will not allow us to see things spiritually because we are alive in the flesh, but when spiritual death happens, a separation—a broken relationship with God—happens, which will remove the scale from our eyes, and we'll see things differently, which will generate fear and lead us to torment.

Many of God's people who can see the dark side will be able to see demons and weird spiritual activities that will traumatize or deceive them to believe that they possess a spiritual gift from God. When such a thing happens, such a person needs prayer to break the stronghold in the name of Jesus Christ. Your eyes are better to stay closed to some things than be opened and aware of things that we don't need to be aware of. God is an all-wise God. He doesn't allow us to view many things around us because observing these things is not good for us while living on earth in the flesh.

God knows, the day you eat of the tree, your eyes shall be open. And ye shall be like gods, knowing good and evil (Genesis 3:5). With the knowledge attained to know good and evil, if we cannot manage such awareness to establish a balance, how can we govern and conduct ourselves responsibly with the realization of unlimited wisdom we have attained, with independence from God? This caused the fall of man.

The man's eyes opened, knowing good and evil but with no wisdom and understanding about evil, unlimited power in the hands of a fool will cause self-destruction and desolation, which resulted in the downfall of man.

> And when the woman saw that the tree was good
> for food and that it was pleasant to the eyes, and
> a tree to be desired to make one wise, she took of
> the fruit thereof, and did eat, and gave unto her
> husband with her; and he did eat. (Genesis 3:6)

All along, the tree was good for food but when God said, "don't touch," did the woman develop a different concept to see the fruit on the tree in a different light? When we have sin and doubt in our heart, if God says "don't touch" we will be like the woman and see the fruit with a different perspective. Because the devil always tries to influence us to see things differently than how we are supposed to see it and understand it.

I call it the second look! You can look at something and admire it for what it is, but when you take your eyes away from it, then relook, you will see it differently.

Now a seed is sown in your conscious and subconscious mind with imaginary thoughts designed to make sense of the image captured—now planted and embedded in your heart, to influence the lustful desires in the flesh, to spring to life and become something more.

The woman now saw the fruit totally different after the enemy tempted her to look at it differently. She was now seeing the fruit with a different pair of eyes, now becoming lust. A desire rooted and lodged in the flesh will produce no good but lead and promote sin and rebellion against God. And it becomes pleasant to the eyes. The eyes is where we can see things and seal images in our conscious awareness. So you can look at something that doesn't really matter, but when the look intensifies with newfound interest associated with wants and desires, it becomes a different look, no more an ordinary look but a look of wanting to have, and that's where lust is born.

Lust is birthed from looking and desiring the thing that we are seeing but cannot have, which begins to manifest in our behavior, choices, even through perception and various other things about life.

One thing I do know about people living in sin, they always seek out accomplices and want others to join in with them. It solidifies their actions to agree with them, to empower their argument, to feel comfortable about what they're doing, to confirm and strengthen their argument.

If no one agrees when somebody is doing wrong, they will not want to do wrong of themselves. Seeking someone to join them in wrongdoing emboldens them and strengthens the wrongdoing they are involved in.

> She took of the fruit thereof, and did eat, and gave also unto her husband with her; and he did eat.

The Bible says, "Out of two or more witnesses shall a word be established." If she had eaten of the fruit alone, nothing possible would have happened. But she got an agreement of two or more witnesses when Adam took and ate of the fruit. That's when the fall was established, and things changed because then their eyes were both open.

There was something new and strange, not the same feelings as before, as if they were both in a different world. So this was not a good thing for their eyes to be open; it was best for their eyes to remain closed from the world. But now they were opened. Open to what? A new reality, new truth, a new dimension with new experiences, and closed off from God's true inspirations, reality, and God's existence.

So their eyes are now open to the world and blinded from God. Therefore, it remains closed from God's presence. Sometimes things that are seen will destroy and break us.

Knowledge is good, but having the right knowledge is best. Things you don't need to know will create problems, ignite fears, and cause hurt and pain. It's good to have understanding and wisdom concerning the thing you're about to realize, so knowledge and wisdom is necessary to guide you so you don't harm yourself. Otherwise, it won't be of any gain.

Moreover, if your eyes are open with no wisdom, knowledge, understanding, discernment, no counsel or power, without the Spirit of God, it will certainly become fruitless and very destructive.

> Adam did eat, and his eyes were opened, and with their eyes both open; noticed they were naked and ashamed.

Knowing that they were naked, a new skill also was developed. They learned how to sew fig leaves to make garments to cover themselves. Yet able to do things different, they became aware of different things, and all this knowledge was not healthy, only separating them from God. All their human faculties and senses had become active; they now could hear God's voice walking in the garden in the cool of the day.

Adam and his wife hid themselves because they were ashamed. Their new-found awareness and understanding were more powerful than their desire to have a closer and more intimate relationship with God.

Adam and his wife should have desired to be in the presence of God, but now being able to see life in a different perspective, everything seemed to be going backwards instead of moving forward. Adam had also changed intellectually, he had developed knowledge of good and evil but it came at a cost. Subtracted from him was the life in God. Spiritual awareness was exchanged for carnality, shame, fear, and everything that is negative and anti-God.

When you listen to the voice of the serpent and you do what the serpent requires of you, your eyes will be opened. When your eyes are open, you're more knowledgeable to what the enemy wants you to see, know, and understand and blocks what God desires to reveal to you. What God wants to show and reveal to you can only be seen when your eyes are closed. With your eyes open, Satan will distract you with enticing pleasures, with things you love and are most vulnerable to, by creating images in your mind to flood your heart to becomes a huge distraction.

Moreover, people who pray with their eyes closed, they don't want to be distracted in worship and praise unto God; a secret moment for revelation and inspiration in order to secure a sound faith in the Lord Jesus Christ. When you get mature in your faith, you pray with your eyes open. Your spiritual depth creates a buffer that guards against any interruptions by you, not seeing what's around you but inside your spirit.

Your focus should be on what you believe in instead of what you're seeing. So you can be looking at something but it's not registering in your mind because your heart is seeing what God wants you to see but that will not be the case when you're not mature and seasoned in the faith.

Adam was afraid when he heard the voice of God walking in the garden. The word of God says, "Adam heard the voice of God walking." That doesn't makes any sense! How can the voice of God be walking? Sin creates confusion with basic knowledge and common sense. Adam had the ability to name all the animals, but now he is having a problem differentiating sounds to discern and make the right judgement in what he was hearing and how it was interpreted. Sin distorts truth and common sense.

The closer God got to Adam, the more he could hear his voice coming closer and closer to him. This was something new to Adam. The spiritual communication between God and Adam was severed because of the fall.

They hid themselves out of fear.

When people begin to turn away from God, they become fearful of His presence by trying to escape because of guilt and shame. Sin precipitates a feeling of nakedness and abandonment.

> And he said, who told thee that thou was naked?
> Hast thou eaten of the tree, whereof I commanded
> thee that thou shouldest not eat? (Genesis 3:11)

When Adam ate of the fruit from the tree, his eyes opened and the Spirit of fear became alive in him. When you become so fearful of God you cannot have a relationship with him, and it also makes you naked and ashamed. Sin unclothed us and made us become ashamed because we are clothed in His righteousness. When we become unclothed and turn away from God, we are now naked from His righteousness. Shame and disgrace will come upon us because we're found to be naked in the spirit.

Naked and ashamed is when our eyes are opened to sin, that causes us to be exposed to things that should not be seen. It only provokes the flesh with torment and fear and all these things can become integrated in our life.

We don't need to know more than what God wants us to know if you don't have wisdom, knowledge, and understanding? A lot of people are so inquisitive about things that don't concern them. If you don't have knowledge and understanding and wisdom; it will go against you, then destroy you. For any information you are getting it is necessary for you to have an understanding about the information and also know how to apply what you are hearing. That is wisdom.

> And the man said, the woman whom thou give to
> be with me, she gave me of the tree, and I did eat.

Adam began to cast blame on the woman. God wants us to be responsible by never shifting blame to someone else. Always stand up to whatsoever the accusation is and face up to it, but cowards always shift the blame by not taking responsibility for their actions.

When we are in trouble with God, He wants us to come and acknowledge our wrongs and ask for forgiveness; but most of the time, people live in denial and shift blame to someone else because they don't want to face up to it, and that is never good. This results in more harm than good.

> And the LORD God said unto the woman, what is
> this that thou hast done?
> And the woman said "The serpent beguiled
> and tricked me, and I did eat," the serpent is now
> at fault.
> And the LORD God said unto the serpent,
> because thou hast done this, thou art cursed
> above all cattle, and above every beast of the field;

upon thy belly shalt thou go, and dust shalt thou
eat all the days of thy life:

Is the serpent the devil or the manifestation in the image of a serpent? The Bible did not state the serpent to be Satan in Genesis.

If we allow things to control and possess our heart, we will be tempted to go against the will of God, and behave differently than we truly are. In such situations, a lot of people commit suicide or do crazy stuff. If not delivered, they will end up very ill because they are susceptible to becoming possessed by evil.

And I will put enmity between thee and the woman, and between thy seed and her seed; it shall bruise thy head, and thou shalt bruise his heel. (Genesis 3:15)

The Lord did not say He is going to put enmity between the man and the serpent. He said He would put enmity between the woman and the serpent, which meant enmity between her seed and the serpent's seed. Who is the seed of the serpent? And who is the seed of the woman?

There is something far more spiritual to be understood. The Bible says "enmity between serpent and the woman" and "between thy seed and her seed." What seed is this of the serpent and what seed is this of the woman? It was revealed to me and to my understanding, the seed of the serpent is a generation of people living in rebellion in the world today. The seed of the woman is the generation of people in God through Christ being born again by faith through baptism and now called the church of the living God.

The seed of the serpent is a nation of people born in rebellion. The seed of the woman are them that are birthed in God's grace, mercy, deliverance, righteousness, and born again believers into the kingdom of God. When the Bible talks about her seed, and the seed of the serpent, it means something.

There was nothing mentioned about the seed of Adam, only the seed of the woman. God did not say Eve because Adam called the woman Eve in her fallen state.

> Unto the woman he said, I will greatly multiply
> thy sorrow and thy conception; in sorrow thou
> shalt bring forth children.

So sorrow and conception go together. You have sorrow in conception, sorrow in other things that are not associated with conception. Is this sorrow in the woman different from the man?

Women tend to be more emotional than men, able to feel *more* sorrow, hurt, pain, stress, strain, worry, and anxiety more than men. Because of the curse of conception pronounced in the Garden of Eden, all the things that surround a woman in their emotions still exist up to this day.

> In sorrow thou shall bring forth children: so, if
> the woman is still having pain in child birth, that
> means the curse of sorrow still exists in her today.

So sorrow is a part of woman's nature. Because it is a curse, that doesn't mean it is demonic. It's natural. When a woman is hurting and feeling pain, it's a natural reaction and cannot be controlled, suppressed, or wished away.

The more men and women understand this known fact, they will be able to cope with these situations, and be more patient and understanding. The more knowledge we get, the more attuned we will be to develop a clearer understanding concerning these conditions, by discerning between the things that are natural from what are illnesses. We can then gain control over this type of sorrow recognized in every woman, by getting the necessary treatment; council, guidance and prayers. Child birth is a known curse associated with sorrow and it is a natural thing that every woman must endure. Although they exist, you can deal with sorrows that are seen in your life if they are a known curse, just like conception conceived in sorrow and giving birth to a child is a known curse.

> And thy desire shall be to thy husband, and he
> shall rule over thee. (Genesis 3:16)

The woman will desire her husband. What about the man desiring his wife? What does it mean that the woman will desire her husband? It means the woman has much deeper feelings for her husband who rarely desires but wants.

Women's emotions are far more in debt than those of men and it's all because of the fall hence a woman will desire far deeper feelings than a man. Desire comes from deep within and is an emotion. A woman will have a more difficult time to govern if her judgment is influenced by feelings and emotions, which are gifts given by God for nurturing, caring and expressing love. Man makes spontaneous decision with very little emotions and can be very much over protective and controlling. This is a sense of security that most women desire, hence he, the husband, will rule over you, his wife.

> And unto Adam, he said, because thou hast hearkened unto the voice of thy wife, and hast eaten of the tree, of which I commanded thee, saying, thou shalt not eat of it: cursed is the ground for thy sake; in sorrow shalt thou eat of it all the days of thy life; (Genesis 3:17) if the man listens to the voice of the woman to disobey the command of God, this means a woman can be more influential than men and have the ability to steer them in a good or destructive path.

Chapter 7

Angels Among Us

P eople have a problem with the existence of angels. They have a problem believing that angels are real and how we exist in this world where there are spiritual beings. We are human beings. That means we have a physical body that enables us to do things in this natural world. We also have a soul and a spiritual man and they operate jointly by communicating with the physical man. Before the fall, our spiritual man was the one in control. He understood God and was able to relate to God and had a relationship with Him.

> Moreover, they heard the voice of the Lord God walking in the garden in the cool of the day. (Genesis 3:8)

The physical man is the host body for the spiritual man, but since the fall and the separation of God from the man, the relationship between the spiritual man and the physical man was altered. The natural man became carnal and became the dominant personality in the human life. Man's five senses became activated to condition his life for earthly experiences and understanding influenced by godly instinct.

We are now more conditioned to interact with and understand the natural world more than the spiritual because our thoughts are what bring about conscious awareness, when our senses become active to be able to interpret and understand our feelings, seeing, hearing, smelling, and tasting. The body becomes more enlightened to the natural world, but not so much the spiritual.

It is challenging living a life without spiritual guidance. To understand and interpret godly things, we need a spiritual connection. So if the Holy Spirit does not lead us, we can be easily deceived and controlled by Satan and his demonic agents that operate in the atmosphere. Most if not all things we experience in the natural world is influenced and related to things happening spiritually, which we are unable to see or understand. We need guidance by the Word of God and inspiration by the Holy Spirit for wisdom to live and strive in a world very active spiritually.

Understanding the movements and behavior of our spiritual man, it will be necessary to be trained to develop discernment and ask God for wisdom.

> If any of you lack wisdom, let him ask of God,
> that giveth to all men liberally, and upbraided
> not; and it shall be, given him. (James 1:5, KJV)

It's complicated to know and understand spiritual encounters because for us, it is a mystery. The devil will take advantage of our ignorance to deceive us to believe lies, make wrong choices, provoke God, be in rebellion against the Word of God and the Holy Spirit of the Lord.

> So, marvel not; for Satan himself is transformed
> into an angel of light. (2 Corinthians 11:14, KJV)

A lot of spiritual communications taking place right now is with fallen angels and demonic entities. One might believe that this is God whom they are talking to, but if we have no understanding and discernment, we will entertain familiar spirits disguising themselves to be inspirational words of God.

In today's world, it becomes challenging to understand and interpret spiritual things with carnal understanding, reasoning, logic and experience compounded by emotions. It requires a relationship with God, guided by the Holy Spirit for wisdom, counsel, and discernment.

To understand things that are happening spiritually, one must be taught and trained how to develop the concepts of believing and understanding spiritual things. In times past, angels were used as messengers from God. Before Jesus Christ came into the world and before the outpouring of the Holy Spirit, angels were used as messengers from God. Angels interacted with man in a natural state. Angels could be seen, spoken to, even touched. After the outpouring of the Holy Spirit, the interaction between man and angels changed. It came to an end.

There is no further need for angels to be messengers to show or give counsel because as Christians, we have a direct line to our Lord and Savior Jesus Christ when we need counsel and guidance. Another reason is that some angels were found to be unfaithful in Genesis 6 before the flood. A third of the angelic host fell with Lucifer from heaven. Many people have a problem, believing that such a thing can indeed happen that an angel can have a relationship with a woman and produce an offspring.

Our social logic and reasoning were never able to make sense of this. However, the Word of God makes it very clear to us that this is entirely possible.

When we look back to one of many scriptures, angels were able to manifest and look like men, behaved like typical men and did things in the natural world such as eat, talk, interact, and make known to man the wisdom of God. They wore garments and looked like ordinary men, but they are spiritual beings.

In Genesis chapter 9, it gives us a foundational understanding concerning angels' association and interaction with a man on earth.

> Moreover, there came two angels to Sodom
> at even, and Lot sat in the gate of Sodom: and
> Lot seeing them rose up to meet them, and he
> bowed himself with his face toward the ground.
> (Genesis 19:1, KJV)

Lot knew what an angel looked like because there was something different and unique about the two men who came to Sodom. He bowed his head in reverence before the two men because he could identify them as angels. However, the people of Sodom were not able to recognize these two men.

So he said, "Behold now, my lords, turn in I pray you, into your servant's house, and tarry all night, and wash your feet." The angels had feet that could be washed and were able to take a nap like any other person.

> So ye shall rise early and go on your ways. Also, they said, Nay; but we will abide in the street all night.

So these angels looked and appeared like ordinary men. You could not tell the difference between them and ordinary men. They were able to manifest and look human. Believers struggle with this subject, of the possibility of angels getting married to women, and giving birth to offspring that became giants. These giants were evil so God destroyed them in the flood, but their wandering souls lives on in the manifestation of the demonic spirits in today's world.

So Lot pressed upon the angels greatly, and they turned in unto him and entered his house, and he made them a feast and did bake unleavened bread, and they did eat (Genesis 19:3). Lot prepared a meal for these two angels to eat; they did eat, and they did drink. That means angels in a human manifestation can wash. They can take a nap or sleep, they can have a conversation with men, they can be touched and be felt. They also can have a meal. They can do everything a man can do.

Before they had gone to bed, all the men from every part of the city of Sodom, both young and old, surrounded the house. The people of Sodom saw two men. They didn't see angels. Lot saw two angels and bowed his head in reverence before them and called them lord.

What was the difference? Why did Lot see two angels, but the men of Sodom saw two ordinary men? When our natural desires spring to life, we want to fulfill these desires, so we cannot see anything beyond our human ability.

The Bible says, we must walk by the Spirit that we don't fulfill the lust in the flesh. Walking by the Spirit will enable us to know spiritual experiences and be a witness for the kingdom of God. Believers, misunderstand the motives of God because they are blinded by their selfish passion and desires. Their human instinct suppresses their spiritual awareness.

Lot had spiritual understanding, not the same mentality of the men in the city, even though he was among them. However, being among them, he was influenced to be dishonest in the presence of the angels. They called to Lot, "Where are the men who came to you tonight? Bring them out to us so that we can have sex with them."

These men were like beasts exhibiting animalistic behavior because they had lost all their human integrity and sensitivity. There are some basic things in life that God makes known to us, easily understood but if we become distracted, it will be so easy for us to be misguided to reshape our now twisted mind that will influence the way we walk, talk, think, and behave.

The people of Sodom began to behave like beasts and in the process had lost their true selves and identity for spiritual guidance and counsel. They would break, disrupt, and destroy anything that came before them without thinking, questioning, or observing.

All the spiritual faculties are locked away, suppressed, and the only thing that will come forth is the beast nature and tendency to devour, control, and destroy. People of God behave differently. They have a calm and humble demeanor, and a person without God always displays anger and rage. Satan will be able to deceive and influence such a one to behave negatively in a hostile environment. Because of the beast nature in man, the spiritual man is unable to be active to bring that person in line with God, who created him in His image and likeness to display the godlike nature.

So the men in Sodom only saw two men; Lot saw two angels. They desired to know, have sex with these men, take advantage of them, display everything associated with the laws of the flesh when it is at work.

> So Lot went out at the door unto them, and shut
> the door after him, and said, I pray you, breth-
> ren, do not so wickedly. Behold now, I have two

daughters which have not known the man; let me, I beg you, bring them out unto you, and do ye to them as is right in your eyes: only unto these men do nothing; for therefore came they under the shadow of my roof. (Genesis 19:6–8)

When you use lies in defense, it has no power. It only ignites and inflames more chaos and problem. The Bible says to know the truth, and the truth will set you free. This fact is what brings about peace. The truth is what also brings deliverance.

When Lot went out and tried to cover up and make good and decided to look good, it only added more fluid to the flames that were already burning. The men of the city became even more desperate, and the evil passion in them became enraged.

So they said, "Stand back. This one fellow came into sojourn, and he will needs be a judge: now will we deal worse with thee, than with them." So they pressed sore upon the man, even Lot, and came near to break the door.

We see that Lot had a good heart, a sound mind, and good intentions. However, it was not right in the things that he was saying. He was defending the angels, who had the power to protect themselves. When we try to secure a case with lies or misinformation, it only creates more problems.

Total surrender is what will be required before God when the situation is getting out of control. There are certain things that we will never have the power to change, and certain times when you have the power—do nothing! It will undoubtedly create more problems, anxiety, stress, and frustration that will lead to destruction.

Similarly, if we can't pay our bills, we will be stressed out, with tension, worry, and anxiety. All these negative things begin to work against us as a tool of the devil to break us, to make us unhappy. Why should we be miserable and unhappy over something that we have no power to change?

It has something to do with our mind, to be in control of every activity around us, based upon our judgment. We have the power of choice. It's called our self-will. However, most of the time, our mind will seize control of the situation, with uncontrollable thoughts influenced by emotions, with a lack of common sense. Every negative emotions within us which makes us vulnerable will ignite a fractured heart imposed by a life of trauma and abuse. With no solutions, the hidden pain is released and expressed as rage.

So we allow our minds to take us for a ride, to become oppressed, depressed by the situation we have no control over.

Lot had no control over the situation. He was trying to do something and only created a problem that was far more uncontrollable, dangerous, and more violent. However, the men put forth their hand and pulled Lot into the house to them and shut to the door.

That means the angels could touch, feel, communicate, talk, take a shower, sleep, and eat. Moreover, these were angels that had the appearance of a man; you will not know the difference. And they smote the men that were at the door of the house with blindness, both small and great: so that they wearied themselves to find the exit.

That means these men who looked like angel, had supernatural powers and abilities to afflict instantaneously evil men, who had the desire to hurt God's people. And the men said unto Lot, "Hast thou here any besides you? Son-in-law and thy sons and thy daughters and whatsoever thou hast in the city, bring them out of this place." However, Lot had previously stated that his daughters knew no man but the angels believed something different. They asked, "Is there any other persons besides sons-in-law?"

Angels have the ability to discern and know of things without being told.

> For we will destroy this place because the cry of them is waxen great before the face of the LORD, and the LORD hath sent us to overthrow it.
>
> Wickedness and evil, are like a cry coming before the Lord, and it comes before the face of God. Whatsoever person does good or evil, God knows; God will always reward anyone for their works whether good or evil.

And Lot went out, and spoke unto his sons in law, which married his daughters, and said, Up, get you out of this place; for the LORD will destroy this city. But he seemed as one that mocked unto his sons in law.

LOT had said earlier that is daughters knew no man, but he went out and spoke to his sons-in-law, who were married to his daughters. However, he said to the men of Sodom outside, his daughters were virgins.

It's always important that we be honest and truthful about any situation. Because God and his angels knew that Lot's daughters were married.

Lot believed the angels that God would destroy the city, but his sons-in-law chose not to believe; it seemed like a joke to them. The Bible says don't be unevenly yoked with unbelievers. Unsaved, unrepented soul of man cannot discern, will not accept, being warned of the dangers that lie ahead. They have no God in them; it's hard for them to understand the things of God, hard for them to believe and to see the move of the Spirit of God.

Lot could see that these men were angels, the men of Sodom saw them as mere men. He understood that God would destroy the city based upon the rebellious behavior of the men in Sodom. So they were blinded by the angels in utter confusions.

Men of evil desires are blinded by uncontrollable anger and rage. Emboldened by foolishness, it is a mockery to them, the things you're able to do and accomplish by faith. It will always be a mockery to them who don't believe, so we must never be offended and take them to task. When people who don't believe in the things that we stand for, by faith, we must not accept or give in to their demands. Even though unpopular, their criticism of you is by reason to make you feel weak and ashamed of the things you believe in and live for.

An evil man will find every excuse not to believe, but to convince himself the obvious is not true. Living in denial will render him powerless and ineffective to make any sound judgment or seek wise counsel even in the moments of desperation. This beastlike tendency is operating in the heart and soul of a wicked man who chooses to live in rebellion against God, cannot understand the truth, but rejects the simple fundamentals about healing, deliverance, and restoration.

Lot had a level of understanding because he was with his half-brother Abraham, who understood and believed in God, and he was a witness of the blessings of Abraham by God. He had an understanding concerning angels' visitations and who angels were. The other men in the city had no clue nor understanding; they only made a mockery of what was happening. And when the morning arose, then the angels hastened Lot, saying, "Arise, take thy wife and thy two daughters, which are here; lest thou consumed in the iniquity of the city."

So the angels stayed with them the entire night while the men in the city, smitten with confusion, were blinded by the angels. So the angels hastened Lot, his wife, and two daughters. However, Lot's sons-in-law stayed because they were unbelievers.

Ungodly people who mock and make fun of believers forces lukewarm Christians to stray from the faith and adopt a more neutral compromised tone. That will serve no purpose but to dishonor God and reinforce the mockery to others in the faith. Be determined to walk and live the gospel with full zeal and vigor. With determination to stand for and defend their faith, God will always favor such a one because the steps of a righteous man are ordered by the Lord and will make perfect his ways.

Of them that are truly ashamed of their faith, and quick to take sides with the world, they don't understand that the basic requirement of the Gospel is your life; for what it's worth, a living sacrifice that should be holy and acceptable to the Lord! For God sees such as reasonable.

There are others who practice their religion by far more discipline, having more conviction than many in the faith. Satan wants to have glory and praise unto himself; he will influence the people of the world to believe lies or distorted truth. However, he will affect you to believe lies concerning your faith, but he will put forth no challenge to those people who serve a false god.

The devil wants you to believe in a false god. But you who serve the only one true and living God will be targeted by the devil. He will try to discourage you through fear and intimidation, causing you to doubt and walk in unbelief. This is the devil's way to neutralize a believer into living a normal, casual sinful life.

Chapter 8

The Origin of the Demonic Spirits

Misguided Concepts

We are battling with forces of darkness that are genuinely beyond us, and many people sometimes, if not all the time, have questions. "Where are these evil spirits coming from, and how are they able to work in, and destroy the lives of so many people. What can we do to overcome them?"

Because of the powers that be, many people don't want to talk about the weird or supernatural experience, even though they desire answers. Or they refuse to engage in any such discussions because of fear and lack of knowledge and ignorance of the truth.

The existence of demonic possessions has been over the years perverted, watered down, misguided, misinterpreted. We don't know what to believe or whom to believe anymore concerning evil spirits and their involvements in this world. The enemy is disguising himself in just about everything, to deceive man to believe a lie and to cause the truth never to be understood, and the main purposes are to deceive man and to have us to believe that what is right is evil and what is evil is good.

We see bad things every day, and because we are exposed to it daily, we become desensitized to it, accepting it to be okay and to be the norm even though we are suffering from its influence.

We accept that bad things are not so bad anymore, and after a while, we begin to accept bad things as truthful. The things that we value as good and trustworthy are diminishing, spoken of as wrong and rejected as lies, not truth and attributes of God designed to build us up.

We find our lives more dark and filled with pain, with no answers to the things that will help us to break free from the conditions that affect us.

Where Demons Come From

Demons are not angels! They are disembodied souls that found no rest in God. They once had a physical body, but God rejected these souls because of their wickedness, rebellion, rejection, and blasphemy of the Word of God. Judgement was passed against them and they became disembodied, now wandering evil spirits.

They have no identity with God, the angels, or with the man's spirit. These souls became wandering souls upon the face of the earth after the flood in the days of Noah.

In Genesis chapter 6:1, the Bible tells us that something was going on in the time of Noah and God was not happy. It came to pass when men began to multiply upon the face of the earth that daughters were born unto them and the Sons of God saw the daughters of men and they were beautiful. This teaching is very controversial to many believers who try to interpret the Bible using their logic, human knowledge, and experience, believing that the sons of God are the sons of Adam and not the angels.

However, if we look in the Word of God, we are called sons of God when we are born again, having acknowledged Jesus Christ as Lord and Savior by faith, baptized and filled with the Holy Spirit. He engrafted us into the olive branch of His kingdom. The kingdom of God was established through the broken body of Jesus Christ; His death, burial, and resurrection. Now we the church are empowered by the Holy Spirit.

We become sons of God through regeneration of our spiritual man, and become alive in God by the Holy Spirit.

There is no evidence in the Old Testament that refers to men being mentioned as the sons of God. The Bible said, "Righteous men of God, holy men of God," never "sons of God." The only one called Son of God is Jesus Christ when He manifested on earth as an angel of the Lord, appearing to Nebuchadnezzar when he cast the three Hebrew boys into the fiery furnace.

Moreover, these three men—Shadrach, Meshach, and Abednego—fell bound into the midst of the burning fiery furnace. "He answered and said, Lo, I see four men loose walking in the middle of the fire, and they have no hurt; and the form of the fourth is like the Son of God" (Daniel 3:23, 25, KJV).

So in the Old Testament, the sons of God are the angels. Angels are spiritual beings; they don't have a physical body. However, they can manifest in the image and likeness of man. In times past, in the scriptures, angels would manifest in the image and likeness of men. In the story of Sodom and Gomorra, when the two angels entered the city, the men in the town believed that they were men. Lot entertained them as angels, gave them food to eat, washed their feet, communicated, talked, and interacted with them.

The men of Sodom saw two men, not two angels, and a desire to use them sexually.

Because angels can manifest to look like men, you cannot tell the difference between an angel and a normal human being. Angels have the same features, but they don't have a soul. They are spiritual beings, no blood in them; the blood is the life of man's soul. So the sons of God came to earth during the time of Noah, and they were able to manifest themselves, to look exactly like humans, and they saw the women and desired for them and took them as wives.

> That the sons of God saw the daughters of men
> that they were fair; and they took them wives of
> all which they chose. (Genesis 6:2, KJV)

The children of the sons of God, they became giants upon the face of the earth.

> There were giants in the earth in those days; and
> also, after that, when the sons of God came in unto

the daughters of men, and they conceive children
to them, the same became mighty men which
were of old, men of renown. (Genesis 6:4, KJV)

So the son of the angels were no ordinary men. These men had
angelic seed in them and possessed not a human spirit because the
human soul can only be inherited through the loins of a man. The
woman was just a carrier for the angelic seed and was able to conceive
and have children with an unknown spirit in a human body. These
unknown spirits became offsprings of the angels. These men that
were born of the woman were neither angels nor human. However,
they now possess an unknown spirit.

So God saw that the wickedness of man was great
in the earth and that every imagination of the
thoughts of his heart was only evil continually. It
repented the Lord that he had made the man on
earth, and it grieved him at his heart. Moreover,
the Lord said, I will destroy man whom I have
created from the face of the earth; both man, and
beast, and the creeping thing, and the fowls of
the air; for it repented me that I have made them.
(Genesis 6:5–7, KJV)

These angels could manifest themselves; they could take on the
shape and look like anything. We would want to believe that angels
are these white winged creatures in the image of a man and beautiful;
that's how we were thought to think.

There are different kinds of angels unknown to us. The angels
that we know of are the ones the scriptures mentioned such as Gabriel,
Michael, and the angel of the Lord. Very few things are mentioned
in the Bible concerning different angels, but angels are very present
among us. We entertain them unaware, not knowing that they are
angels because we don't have that instinctive spiritual eyes to be able
to see and understand that these are angels living amongst us.

They don't have the power to do anything as we would want to believe, unless on assignment being in the presence of God. So these men, offspring of the angels, were giants upon the face of the earth. In those days, they did not possess the spirit of a man or spirit of an angel. The Bible recognizes them as an evil spirit.

So when the flood came upon the face of the earth, many, if not all of these humans that had an angelic spirit in them died out in the flood. However, their spirit lives on. These wandering spirits, also known as demons are roaming upon the face of the earth, seeking a host body to possess.

We see all kinds of evil upon the face of the earth, for reference:

> For there are certain men crept in unawares, who were before of old ordained to this condemnation, ungodly men, turning the grace of our God into lasciviousness, and denying the only Lord God, and our Lord Jesus Christ. (Jude 1:4, KJV)

We need to go back to where it all started, the old landmark of our faith, to recognize the truth of the word because, over the centuries, the Word of God became perverted and diluted, and not having the strength and the power because of so many different interpretations. There are false preachers and misguided believers on assignment by the devil, preaching and formulating doctrines to deceive Christians to believe lies. However, the truth is in the Word of God by the revelation of the Holy Spirit.

For there were certain men crept in unawares who were before of old, ordaining to this condemnation, ungodly men turning the grace of God into lasciviousness and denying the only wise God: the Lord Jesus Christ.

Certain men creep in unawares. Who are these men? How were they able to come in unaware? These are the same men of old mentioned in Genesis 6, the souls that died in the flood. The spirits of the giant that found no rest in God became wandering spirits, now demons by name. Searching for a host body, they will enter in, seize control of the life and body of any person living in sin, and in total rebellion against God.

Your life, body, and soul can be possessed by these evil spirits. They will also occupy your home, car, animals, and everything exposed to them. These evil spirits, demons by name, are like parasites. They feast on our emotions, they attack our bodies causing chronic illnesses and diseases and they cause emotional, psychological, mental and physiological pain and suffering. Their sole purpose is to control you and their common goal is to destroy humanity.

Fallen angels are not able to possess a human body because they have a spiritual body. They can influence, manipulate, dictate, oppress, vex, afflict, and control our thought through temptation by inducing fear when men begin to walk away from God.

When men choose not to listen, obey, and follow the counsel of God, they can be possessed by evil spirits. There are various type of demonic spirit that the Lord showed to me some time ago in a dream, and I called these types "airborne spirits."

Years ago, when the Lord called me to the deliverance ministry, He showed me in a vision how a human can be possessed by an evil spirit. It was about 4:00 a.m. that I had this vision. I could see an image of a person. I heard the Spirit of the Lord say, "Look and observe what's happening."

I could see with an understanding beyond me an image of a person entertaining a thought induced through temptation. The thoughts could be to entertain lustful thoughts, get angry, hold on to unforgiveness, and stay bitter. In entertaining those thoughts, I could see in my dream something forming like a cloud, a misty figure. It had no defined shape, hovering over the head of the image of the person. The cloudy misty image was entertained by the person. It had no personality; it had no name. It was neutral.

The heart of the person created that cloudy misty figure around themselves, and when they entertained the induced thoughts, that misty figure entered into the body of the person. I could supernaturally see this, how it lodged in the chest area of the person and began to take the shape or form of whatever the thought entertained.

If that thought is lust, hurt, pain, unforgiveness, it begins to take on the form of the induced idea entertained, feeding the misty figure to it a personality. It begins to grow and develops personalities exhibiting anger, hurt, pain, or sorrow. When it takes on or impersonate the temptation, personality traits such as anger, hurt, pain, sorrows, and traumas can influence your conscious or subconscious mind and become a stronghold.

Moreover, the Lord was saying to me in the vision, "An airborne spirit somewhat is different from the souls perished in the flood." Lost souls with no spirit identity but with spirit personality, are possessing and afflicting men through fear and intimidation.

So there are various type of demonic spirits. That is unknown to us, and God doesn't require us to know and to understand. All these evil spirits see we can be easily influenced and corrupted by them. So they camouflage themselves in various area of our lives where we are most vulnerable and susceptible to them. However, we can recognize and discern their behaviors and activities by the leading of the Holy Spirit by their manifested fruit. We have the authority through Christ to rebuke, bind, and cast the evil spirit out of the soul of a person, object, or things in the name of Jesus Christ.

There is something also we need to understand. There are few times that Satan or demons are mentioned in the Old Testament. When mentioned, it is done so in a subtle way, by warning and instructing man to avoid evil.

Before the coming of Jesus Christ, Satan had the authority, and no one dared challenge him because he was the head of all principalities and powers, and God recognizes spiritual governance. He was first mentioned and exposed as an enemy by Jesus Christ. Jesus Christ came into this world as the Son of the living God, the Light of the world, the conquering Lion of the tribe of Judah, King of all kings and Lord of our Lords. He came to set the captives free.

Filled with the Holy Spirit, when John baptized him, he was led by the Holy Spirit into the wilderness to be tempted by the devil. When He overcame the temptation, that's when the ministry of Jesus Christ began to teach, reveal and expose the works, operations, and influence of demonic spirits and the kingdom of darkness ruled by Satan.

Preaching the kingdom of heaven is at hand. That is the gospel for the church, the body of Jesus Christ His mission and purpose was to destroy the works of darkness.

Fallen angels are very much amongst us. Also understand that the restrainer, the Holy Spirit, forbade them from interacting with men. So it is prohibited by God for us to communicate or form any bonds and relationship with entities. It can become very dangerous for our well-being and prosperity in this world.

Jesus Christ has seized all power, dominion, and control over Satan through the cross, so he has no more power over us. The energy that he has is the power we have given unto him when we are in total rebellion against God. We give Satan legal rights to take control over our families and us when we are in rebellion against God.

There is a seed that has been sown in the life of man from the beginning. God tells the man Adam, "The tree of knowledge of good and evil, don't you touch or eat from it." The man ate of the fruit of knowledge of good and evil. While knowledge of itself is not evil, we must also understand that good doesn't destroy evil; good overcomes evil.

Evil destroys the wicked. Evil existed before Satan. God said in his word, He created good, and He created evil. Evil is a tool used by God for His wrath and judgment to accomplish His purpose for good.

> If that nation, against whom I have pronounced,
> turn from their evil, I will repent of the evil that I
> thought to do unto them. (Jeremiah 18:8)

God's people need to renew their mind. Satan is not God's opposite. God has no opposite; Satan is the opposing force to humanity.

God sent an evil spirit upon Saul when he was in total disobedience and rebellion against God. He also posted a lying spirit in the mouths of the prophet. You may want to believe that the evil spirit sent to torment Saul, and the lying spirit in the mouth of the prophets, was Satan himself. No, it was not. Satan is a fallen angel. Evil is a spirit of God. Satan became the embodiment of evil because of the fall. He is the first fallen. Everything that falls after him is under his authority and control.

Satan is an official name given to all the fallen angels and demons. His power and authority have nothing to do with him but gained through his position being the prince of darkness. He is not omnipresent, he is unable to be many places at the same time. It took only one angel in Revelation to bound Satan and cast him in the bottomless pit.

> And I saw an angel come down from heaven, having the key of the bottomless pit and a great chain in his hand. And he laid hold on the dragon, that old serpent, which is the Devil, and Satan, and bound him a thousand years. And cast him into the bottomless pit, and shut him up, and set a seal upon him, that he should deceive the nations no more, till the thousand years should be, fulfilled: and after that, he must be, loosed a little season.

So when someone is being afflicted by a devil or by Satan, the affliction does not come from the same spirit. These attacks come from various evil spirits, all representing the chief of the fallen: Satan. The fallen angels, demonic spirits, airborne spirits all operate in the kingdom of darkness to accomplish evil.

When we rebuke the devil, we rebuke Satan. This doesn't necessarily mean that that is *the* Satan called Lucifer who is the first fallen. All the fallen angels are chained in darkness and would never be able to be exposed to the light of God. They all have the same agenda, which is to do evil. Evil shall destroy the wicked. Wickedness is in the heart of man. They desire to do evil continuously.

Because they are out of the will of God, the evil that influences the wicked heart to accomplish every wicked imagination of the heart, shall turn around to destroy the wicked. That same evil will destroy Satan, the fallen angels, and the demonic spirits at the end of the world in the lake of fire.

In Revelation, the Bible says that hell, death, the grave, the false prophets and Antichrist will all be cast into the lake of fire. The Bible did not mention that evil will be cast in the lake of fire. This may be controversial, but evil is a spirit used as a tool by God to accomplish His purpose, will, and judgment. Evil is also used as a weapon for war against the enemies of God to establish law and order (something to think about, requires godly wisdom).

Good only bring about peace. Good can never bring about destruction, can never bring about chaos, can never bring about desolation when God is in his wrath and his anger. With the sins that is upon the face of the earth, the Bible says, "If God doesn't judge the inhabitants of the world the inhabitants thereof won't know His righteousness."

When God unleashed His anger, evil is what is unleashed upon a rebellious nation to accomplish peace, righteousness, and fear of God. In the heart of the wicked, God must and shall be feared. The more we understand the truth, the more we have power for freedom.

Know the truth, and the truth will set you free. The demons of today are not fallen angels. The demonic spirits of today are wandering souls from the souls that died in the flood and found no rest in God. These spirits, according to Jude crept in unaware. The men of old and they are living in us today, in the body of men who are rebelling against God, fulfilling their evil and wicked desires. And we only can overcome them through the power of the blood, the authority of the cross because in so doing, we have victory in the name of Jesus Christ.

We have victory, and we must exercise our victory in Jesus Christ because He is the Son of the living God, the Author and finisher of our faith, our rock and shield and hiding place. Praise the Lord!

Chapter 9

The Power of the Cross

We must apply the Word of God wherever we go and in whatever we do. It's always necessary that we live the Word of God, know the truth, and the truth will set you free, the truth associated with the Word of God.

With our new life in Christ as Christians, we truly don't know the power we possess and the abilities that we can exhibit in and through our life by faith. God took great pleasure when he created man. He formed the beasts of the field from the dust of the ground, but when it came to creating man, God said, "Let us make man in our image."

The man was the only created being or creature formed by God; He stooped down and formed man from the dust of the ground. He truly loves man and took pleasure in forming the body of the man for His purpose.

> Having predestinated us unto the adoption of children by Jesus Christ to himself, according to the good pleasure of his will. (Ephesians 1:5)

So the Son of God was given a body to live and exist on earth. When the Word became flesh, He walked on earth in the body of a man, Christ Jesus. He was then put to death and raised by the power of the Holy Spirit. When the woman saw him the morning of the resurrection and was about to touch him, he said, "Woman, don't touch me. I have not ascended to the Father yet."

The Father glorifies the Son in His new and final resurrected body. The same state will be inherited by the saints, they who are redeemed and cleansed by the blood of Jesus Christ.

The Bible says, "At the last trump of God, the dead in Christ shall rise first, and they who are alive, will be transformed and caught up to meet the Son of Man in the air, and we shall be like him, taking on his likeness" (1 Thessalonians 4:16–17).

He came in our image and likeness so we can be transformed in His glorified state. The body that we are in right now will be discarded. This body was cursed since the fall of Adam. Jesus became a curse for us to redeemed man and, in the process of redemption, destroy the works of darkness. That was the purpose of the Son of God manifested in the sinful flesh to destroy the works of darkness. We must understand that something happened in the first world. Darkness, destruction, and desolation were upon the face of the earth, which annihilated all living creatures from the surface of the planet.

But God had a plan to restore life on earth in a new way.

He chose to use man whom He had formed powerfully to bring about once more holiness and righteousness on earth. The man whom He created was perfect but had to go through the transitional process by his own choice to morph into a new image.

God allowed man to fall by his own choice. Somehow it seemed man would be unredeemable based on the rebelliousness of man's nature. The Bible says when sin abounds, grace abounds far beyond every sin that man could have ever committed to bring them back onto Himself.

There are no sins that man could ever commit that God will not forgive. Man also had to go through the life experience of Christ as a road map to victory by bearing their cross of suffering.

> For if we have been planted together in the likeness of his death, we shall also be in the image of his resurrection. (Roman 6:5)

Man's pain and sufferings merge into the life of Jesus Christ through His death, burial, and resurrection power of God, through the baptism of the Holy Spirit.

Now, if we try to understand the wisdom of God employing our human intellect and reasonings, it will be foolishness to us. The Bible says the stupidity of the cross is the wisdom of God. So the unveiling of the mystery of God for salvation is deliverance and restoration of fallen man by way of the cross.

Jesus Christ came in the likeness of sinful flesh. He had no sin in Him, lived a sinless life which teaches us about the kingdom of God in parables of human knowledge.

Thy Kingdom Come

Thy kingdom come represents the crucified body of Jesus Christ, raised from the dead by the power of the Holy Spirit. It was revealed unto me that this present state of Jesus Christ represents the third-dimensional man.

Christ came to establish a new kingdom in Himself because the world was corrupted and destined for destruction. This present earth, He rebuilt and restored by the spoken *Word*. He came to destroy this world and all its creations that were corrupted, controlled, and enslaved by the devil. So the things that seem very foolish to us is the wisdom of God, by way of the cross to give us a new life in Himself, but we had to give up our life to obtain His life.

> Therefore, if any man is in Christ, he is a new creature: old things passed away; behold, all things become new. (2 Corinthians 5:7)

To be birthed into the kingdom of God can only be attained through Christ by totally surrendering our life to him.

> That if thou shalt confess with thy mouth the Lord Jesus, and shalt believe in thine heart that

God hath raised him from the dead, thou shall;
be saved. (Roman 10:9)

And in so doing, we attain a new life because we were under the
control of darkness and the evil one.

Not by works of righteousness which we have
done, but according to his mercy he saved us, by
the washing of regeneration, and renewing of the
Holy Ghost. (Titus 3:5)

The fall of man was ordained and necessary for us to transition
out of this world and present life. We must be born again in total
brokenness and surrender to Jesus Christ as our Lord and Savior.
Repent from all your sins, shortcomings, failures, selfish desires. To
be made whole by His grace and mercy, choose and be determined to
walk and live a holy, righteous, and godly life. Forgive others, most
of all yourself. Be baptized and filled with God's Holy Spirit and His
fruit.

Cast your burdens, fears, hurts, and pains to the Lord in
exchange for the life of Christ for the forgiveness of all our sins. "For
he hath made him be sin for us, who knew no sin; that we might be
made the righteousness of God in him." When we live in this life, we
are under the control mechanism of the law that governed sin. But
when we die to this life, we are under the guidance of the law of the
Spirit.

For the law of the Spirit of life in Christ Jesus
hath made me free from the law of sin and death.
(Roman 8:2)

As a reference, a person now dead is no longer responsible for
past life experiences, not responsible for their bills, the covenant of
marriage no longer binding. Everything associated with his life ends.
The same is symbolic in the realm of the spirit for them who are born
again.

God knows the life we're living, but by His grace and mercy, the love of God concerning, being dead in Christ means you are no longer responsible for what happened in your past life when you were unsaved and lived in the world.

> Therefore, if any man is in Christ, he is a new creature: old things passed away; behold, all things become new. (2 Corinthians 5:17)

So when you are raised in Christ, it represents being born again. Jesus Christ forgives, cleanses, and washes you in His blood; that is symbolic of God's forgiveness for you to become a new person in God.

Only through faith are we able to see, believe, and experience the revolutionary change in our life. The problem is, many people are not willing to understand or accept the truth. God does not see us in the way we see ourselves. If the Word of God says we are redeemed and cleansed by the blood of the Lamb, that's the way He views us. Despite all our failures, past never-ending mistakes, and difficulties, He sees us no different. In reference, when God took the rib of the man and formed woman and brought her to the man and married them, they become one flesh in the eyes of God.

So we need to see things the way God sees it, appreciating the Word of God for what it says, training our mind to accept and believe, so that faith can spring to life for us to bear fruit unto God to be able to love and appreciate others and ourselves. He loves and appreciates us but so many things can cause us to lose hope and feel discouraged and hate ourselves.

Christ Put to Death

God doesn't want us to see things how the world presents it, nor fulfill the lustful desires of the flesh but to walk by faith and not by sight. There are many things in the world that will influence us to believe lies, distorted truths, and discourage us to lose faith and hope, to doubt the Word of God. It takes determination with endurance to come into the fullness of the knowledge and understanding of God, and to be used by Him powerfully.

He wants us to see and interpret and understand what Jesus Christ has done for us when He gave Himself as a living sacrifice to be crucified on the cross. The enemy thought that He had victory over the Son of the living God.

Carrying the cross on His way to be crucified, evil men mocked, jeered, spat upon him, scourged him. They did everything that was so evil and wicked. They celebrated and even exchanged a thief for the Son of man, with chants, "Give us Barabbas and away with Jesus." Jesus was not guilty of any of the charges made against him.

> Let Christ the King of Jews, come down from the
> cross that we may see and believe. (Mark 15:32)

They that were there to watch Him be crucified reviled Him. One of the thieves who was to be crucified reviled Him. The cross has everything to do with our faith walk, and it is a sacrifice, a burden we all must carry. Many will ridicule, hate, and despise you for your faith, see you like a nobody, not worthy to live. Jesus Christ took the sins and burdens upon His shoulder, thorns on His head, breaking every curse known and unknown to man. He was despised and rejected by men; a man of sorrows and acquainted with grief, and we hid as it were our faces from Him. He was hated, and we esteemed Him not.

> Surely, he hath borne our griefs and carried our
> sorrows: yet we did esteem him stricken, smitten
> of God, and afflicted. However, he's wounded for
> our transgressions; he was bruised, for our iniqui-
> ties: the chastisement of our peace was upon him,
> and with his stripes, we all healed. (Isaiah 5:3–5)

He was carrying the load of the sin of man upon His back, but they didn't know that he was on His way to victory. They didn't know it because it seemed to them He was at His weakest moment. However, that was the moment of power when Jesus Christ carried His cross on His shoulders. Each step He made was a step closer to victory, a step closer to defeating the prince of darkness, Satan.

In the eyes of the disciples, they saw defeat and failure. In the eyes of the Pharisees they wanted to see him dead. And in the eyes of the principalities and powers, they saw victory over God.

A man at his weakest moments, about to die, not to exist anymore, this must be it!

But they didn't know that was a part of the plan of God to victory, Jesus Christ nailed to the cross. He asked for water, and they gave Him vinegar to drink. He suffered on the cross, in pain and agony.

When Jesus Christ was about to give up the spirit, He said, "Father, forgive them for they know not what they had done." God the Father, God the Son, knew what would happen. Evil and darkness knew not. It seemed foolish to them, who thought that they had victory when Christ gave up the ghost and died.

The kingdom of darkness, the prince of darkness, the powers that rule over the atmosphere realized then that they had made a big mistake. A significant breach was committed in their kingdom. When night came over and covered the entire earth, there was an earthquake, a shaking. Something was wrong. They allowed a righteous man, without sin, to die.

The Bible says the wages of sin is death. There was no sin committed by the Son of man. So there was a breach in the law of sin, death, hell, and the grave. A righteous soul was in darkness, and it never should have happened. What happened next? The gates of hell were shaken, the kingdom of the underworld began to shake, and in the process, the devil was overthrown because of the breach in the realm of darkness.

God overthrew the devil from within. He who had committed no crimes and had no sin became sin for us, and because of that, a breach occurred in the kingdom of darkness. The devil was overthrown and defeated, without a fight. This makes the resurrection of God so powerful. The Spirit of God raised Christ from the dead. The grave could not restrain Him; He had to be raised and given back life. So the power of the resurrection shook the gates of hell, and He defeated and overthrew the enemy in the process. The kingdom of darkness became the kingdom of the Son of man.

> And the seventh angel sounded; and there were great voices in heaven, saying, the kingdoms of this world have become the kingdoms of our Lord, and of his Christ, and he shall reign forever and ever. (Revelation 11:15)

We have no idea how powerful we are. We have no idea how much the cross meant for us, and a lot of us are afraid to be identified with God, ashamed to be associated with the things of God.

Jesus Christ overthrew the kingdom of darkness through the power of the resurrection. The word of God would have no meaning or any power if Christ had not risen from the dead. We have unlimited power because of Christ. We are now in Him. The things required of us is to live a life holy and acceptable to the Lord.

The devil wanted to fulfill the pride in his heart to be like the Most High God, to ascend above the heavens and become like God, but the resurrection power of Jesus Christ dethroned his ability and desire, and he is now defeated by the King of kings and Lord of lords.

Chapter 10

The Seven Spirits of the Lord

G od is amazing; He is the Author and the Finisher of our faith, our rock, shield, and hiding place.

> Moreover, out of the throne proceeded lightning and thundering and voices: and there were seven lamps of fire burning before the throne, which are the Seven Spirits of God. (Revelation 4:5)
>
> Also, there shall come forth a rod out of the stem of Jesse, and a Branch shall grow out of his roots: Moreover, the Spirit of the LORD shall rest upon Him, the Spirit of Wisdom and Understanding, the Spirit of Counsel and Might, the Spirit of Knowledge and the Fear of the LORD. (Isaiah 11:1–2)

There are seven spirits of God, the same Spirit of different manifestation: the Spirit of the Lord, the Spirit of Wisdom, the Spirit of Understanding, the Spirit of Counsel, the Spirit of Might, the Spirit of Knowledge, and the Spirit of Fear of the Lord.

As Christians, we must be operating in the seven spirits of the Lord.

The Holy Spirit

The Holy Spirit of God causes us to bear nine fruits associated with God's holy requirements.

> The Fruit of the Spirit is love, joy, peace, longsuf-
> fering, gentleness, meekness, goodness, faith, and
> temperance. (Galatians 5:22)

The Holy Spirit is our seal of identification, a brand associated with a relationship through the regeneration of our spirit, the day we know and come to accept Jesus Christ as Lord and Savior. He is our Comforter, given unto us to abide with us forever, and the Spirit of Truth that guides and reveals the Word of God to make it practical.

The Holy Spirit manifests in the outpouring of the Holy Ghost for the empowerment of the body of Christ for religious purposes: nine gifts associated with the Holy Ghost for the emancipation of the church.

> To each is given the manifestation of the Spirit
> for the common good. (1 Corinthians 12:7)

There are nine gifts of the Spirit: word of wisdom, word of knowledge, discernment of Spirit, the gift of prophecy, gift of faith, the gift of healing, working miracles, diverse kinds of tongues, and interpretation of tongues. For the building up and empowerment of the church of the living God, the nine gifts of the Spirit demonstrate that the one true and living God is very present with us.

The Spirit of Counsel

Not many people like receiving counsel and they get offended when they receive counsel. The prideful person is never willing to receive counsel and submit willingly to authority. Counsel gives us guidelines to keep us in line, restrain us from ego and temper, and allow us to make wise judgments in decision-making.

Required are your obedience and total surrender of your self-will to God's Word, laws, and principles, for blessings and prosperity, good health, and strength.

The Spirit of Might

It is that ability you have in God to do things beyond you, not because you are strong. It's the ability to do something, to find that extra drive that you never knew or thought was there to take you across the finish line.

> I can do all things through Christ, which strengthens me. (Philippians 4:13)

The Spirit of Might, the enabling power that gives you confidence, happens when you lose hope against all the odds and conditions that make you feel hopeless. When you say to yourself, "I can do this!" it triggers something in you and gives you the strength and the ability to go beyond you. Then you realize it's not you, but it is God. Your strength is not determined by your physical ability but by your spiritual stability.

The Spirit of Knowledge

Due to the lack of knowledge, God's people perish.

> The heart of the prudent gets; and the ear of the wise seeks knowledge. (Proverbs 18:15)

Education is important. A man of knowledge increases in strength. Knowledge gives confidence with self-awareness.

Truth keeps knocking at our door, but we keep letting lies and deceits in. Who will benefit the most when in doubt? The evil influences and questionable decisions you make when in doubt. We must desire the knowledge of God.

> Study to show thyself approved unto God, a workman that needs not to be ashamed, rightly dividing the word of truth. (2 Timothy 2:15)

The Spirit of Understanding

In the lips of him that hath understanding, wisdom exists. However, there is a spirit in man, and the inspiration of the Almighty giveth them understanding.

Understanding is always associated with truth, and the truth is the pillar of a sound foundation that will bring about changes in our most difficult moments and situations. One's joy, happiness, and well-being happen when understanding is at its fullness. It alleviates stress and strain when under pressure.

Some of the problems we are carrying have to do with our ignorance of not knowing the solution to the problem, and possibly resolved by a simple solution. Without understanding, it becomes a mountain, wall, and roadblock for a breakthrough to achieve success.

Whenever we feel inspired, understanding will enable us to make a wise judgment. The enemy will not be able to distort or manipulate your mind to doubt your actions to fulfill the inspiration of God. We must seek out and search for understanding concerning the things of God. There are so many people who are living in defeat, because they are without knowledge. Understanding your knowledge requires wisdom. Wisdom has to do with the application, to apply knowledge. Many Christians' knowledge of God is based on how they were taught the Word of God in their faith journey. However, they have no personal conviction and personal experience to understand about the ways, nature, and will of God concerning their lives.

The Spirit of Fear of the Lord

In anything that you do, you must have the holy fear of God because the fear of God is the beginning of wisdom. The fear of God promotes a holy reverence for worship, a recipe for a healthy relationship and fellowship with God.

Let us hear the conclusion of the whole matter: Fear God and keep his commandments:

for this is the full duty of man. (Ecclesiastes 12:13)

The Spirit of Fear is entirely different from the fear that is generated from your emotions. Emotional fears generated by an evil influence is a tool the devil uses to afflict, control, manipulate, and destroy the people of God. For God has not given us that Spirit of Fear, but love power and a sound mind. "O fear the LORD, ye his saints: for there is no wants to them that fear Him." This Spirit of Fear in the heart of God's people opened doors for blessings, provision, safety, and compassion. Godly fear provokes God, the mighty warrior, to our defense and protection.

The Spirit of Wisdom

If any of you lack wisdom, let him ask of God, that giveth to all men liberally, and upbraided not; and it shall be given unto him. (James 1:5)

Experience teaches wisdom and wisdom only comes from God. It grows with us. When developed, if carefully nurtured by faith, it bears fruits that will enrich us to create a positive mind and attitude, which we will be able to use to make a right judgment for peace and happiness.

However, the wisdom that is from above is first pure, then peaceable, gentle, and easy to be intreated, full of mercy and good fruits, without partiality, and without hypocrisy. (James 3:17)

Guided by Quick Understanding

Moreover, shall make him of quick understanding in fear of the LORD: and he shall not judge

after the sight of his eyes, neither reprove after
the hearing of his ears. (Isaiah 11:3)

However, we must be aware of two things here. We must take note of our eyes and what we see, which is our visual. It is also essential for us to protect our ears, and the things we hear or listen to. Most of the time, when people become possessed by evil influences, it has to do with what they are listening to through their ear gate and by the things they see through their visual or eye gate.

Most people in today's world are guided by what they see and what they hear. These two senses stimulate and affect our judgment and emotional decisions. The way we see things and how we interpret it and what we understand and how we evaluate it will influence your perspective. Depending on the condition of your heart, even the right situations can be devastating and terrible.

Not everything that we see should be interpreted to be true, or things that you hear should be perceived to be right. Seeing something you never intended to see, it enters your spirit or subconscious mind. When you take a second look, it becomes a look with intent. How you look at it then will register in your conscious thoughts, your memory.

Same with the things you hear or listen, or hearing something you do not intend to understand. It registers in the subconscious mind. When you choose to listen, it now becomes intentional. Your self-will is expressed in your conscious mind.

I remember some time ago, I used to sleep with my TV and radio turned on. One night I was wrestling in my sleep and woke up. The radio was on a Christian station in the night. A specific type of music was playing, and in my subconscious mind, I was dreaming and experiencing what I heard in my sleep. Whatsoever was in that music, it came out into my subconscious mind, and I was there wrestling with something that was coming from the music through my ear gate.

However, every man is tempted, when he's drawn
away of his lust and enticed. Then when lust hath
conceived, it bringeth forth sin: and sin, when it
is finished, bringeth forth death. (James 1:14–15)

The devil will also manipulate your thoughts visually, so the same things you see and analyze, he can influence you into seeing them as a means of temptation, which will lead into sin, which becomes demonic bondage if not delivered.

How you apply yourself in a righteous and in a holy way, and how you conduct your life with restraint, the fruit of the spirit— meekness, temperance, patience, self-control—all these things come through the fear of God and will lead, guide, and empower you in your choices and decision-making. What you see and what you hear associated with evil influences will never be able to gain access to your soul when you stay committed to the word of God.

Quick understanding is a manifestation of all Seven Spirits of the Lord. It is that ability in the spirit to make a spontaneous decision or judgment concerning any matter without thinking to discern the outcome. Each manifestation protects you from the evil seed of influence, popup thoughts, the subtle craft of the devil to seduce your mind.

> Keep your heart with all diligence; for out of it
> are the issues of life. (Proverbs 4:23)

Quick understanding is associated with what not to listen to, or if you do, it will be filtered out. It will not be allowed into your soul, only the fear of God will occupy your soul. You will not do certain things and behave in ways that go against the principles and teaching concerning the laws of God.

To abide in His presence and fulfill His laws is to stay under the shadows of the Almighty. Based upon the things you see and the things that you hear, you would have a quick understanding and quick discernment. We cannot be slow in our approach because evil darts will always be coming against us.

We must be on the alert, and make precise and accurate judgments. We don't know what form the enemy will come in. The devil comes in all manner of different ways, so we must have this mindset that he is out to get us, and we cannot allow ourselves to be laid back or lukewarm. The thing we love the most is always the thing that will be used against us the most. This is a common tactic used by the devil.

> Walk in the Spirit, and ye shall not fulfill the lust of the flesh. (Galatians 5:16)

The devil disguises himself or camouflages himself in the things that we pay little attention to and the things we love and trust the most is how we get caught into the traps set for us. We freely allow and embrace the things we love and adore, no matter what. We must be able to walk away for Christ.

Many people have a problem in coming to Christ. They cannot walk away; they cannot give up the things they do, love, and cherish—not knowing that when you give up something for Christ, you get more in return.

> Moreover, Jesus answered and said, Verily I say unto you, no man hath left the house, or brethren, or sisters, or father, or mother, or wife, or children, or lands, for my sake, and the gospel. However, he shall receive a hundredfold now in this time, houses, and brethren, and sisters, and mothers, and children, and lands, with persecutions; and in the world to come eternal life. (Mark 10:28–29)

What happened to Lot's wife? She could not walk away without looking back, and her heart was into substance, temporary things, that don't mean anything worth giving up your life for. We must be able to walk away for Christ.

> Cast all your cares upon Him; because he cares for you. (1 Peter 5:7)

When we think that we are standing tall, all our supports and everything else can quickly disappear. Our friends can abandon us, and our property and wealth can disappear in an instant. Rich at eleven, poor by noon. We are left standing with absolutely nothing.

The word of God clearly says, "He will never leave you, nor will he ever forsake you." You cannot go according to the things that you hear or the things that you see. You need to have quick judgment, quick discernment in your understanding to make the necessary analysis and decisions. We need the Spirit of God. Having no fear for God, we will carelessly do things, or say things in a carefree way.

When we know God will judge, chastise, and break us when we find ourselves at a place where no one can see us, the fear for God cautions us to know, He's watching.

Chapter 11

Breaking Your Chains

W e were born in sin, and it has nothing to do with you. It has nothing to do with me; it has nothing to do with your parents. We were born in sin! Moreover, we are made cursed in this flesh.

The flesh is your physical body, and its natural desires can never please God. If you present your fleshly desires to Him, He will reject it. No matter how good you are, how clean you walk, without making mistakes, your flesh will never please God in this body.

Flesh and blood can never inherit the kingdom of God. It was rejected the day Adam fell from God's presence. Moreover, from that day to present, man has been living in a fallen state. The Bible was clear that Adam was born a human flesh, and the second man Adam a quickening spirit.

Jesus Christ is that second Adam. We are in the kingdom of God through Christ, through saying we believe in God and confessing that Jesus Christ is the Son of the living God.

We were born into this world through the seed of Adam. However, by choice we are rebuilt, reformed, and renewed by faith and sincere confession. We become accepted into the kingdom of the second man Adam.

In our day-to-day life we have choices, and we are responsible for the decisions made. There are things in life we have no power over or no control. There are some things about the human makeup that Satan can tap into and be able to control and manipulate our mind and our body.

As a child growing up, we make individual decisions, not the decisions we would have made if there was not a devil; but since there is a devil, we made bad choices because of ignorance and lack of knowledge. When we make these choices, and it comes to pass, it leaves us with scars.

We have a lot of these scars in our life, and some of these scars are truly deep, and it goes intense even in our subconscious mind. We have so many questions. Why? Why is this thing happening and keeps on repeating itself? What can I do to resolve all these things that are happening to me? Some of these things we have no answer for, some of the thoughts, you have no control over. It comes forcibly, and it comes with controlling mechanics that you cannot shake off yourself and requires spiritual intervention and prayers from the saints washed in the blood of Jesus Christ.

So we look at these things as spiritual chains in our lives that hold us hostage to our past, hostage to our failures, and hostage to our pains in so many ways. How can we identify these chains? What can we do to break it from our lives and free ourselves from the constant onslaught and affliction from the enemy?

Because we are unable to see the devil at work in our misfortunes, what I'm seeing is people at work, fulfilling the purposes and will of the devil.

I see things happening around me. What's causing them to happen? What gives them life? I am doing things to myself that is endangering my life, future, and relationships with families and friends.

Why am I going against the laws of God? When God speaks to us through His Word, that if we sin against Him by breaking the law, these are the things that would happen to us. We see these things happening yet despite the warning signs we continue down the path of destruction. This thing will confuse us to the point that thoughts will spring in our mind, to the point that we start saying stupid things to ourselves for example, "I am no different from the person committing sins because it appears my life is worse off than that man who is living in sin." I am loving God, and I have bad experiences. God, we need your understanding!

For us to live, strive, and prosper as children of God in this world, our spiritual man must live and express himself within us. Is sown a natural body, raised a spiritual body. There is a physical body, and there is a spiritual body (1 Corinthians 15:44).

Also, if you are in the flesh, you will always have problems in this body of rebellion that is full of every evil work of darkness. However, still, we need this body to exist. The Bible says, we must put this flesh under subjection, that the spiritual man can spring to life and expresses himself in God in this world.

However, a lot of us don't even know how to walk by the spirit and how to express ourselves in the Spirit. We don't even know how to pray in the anointing. Things concerning the faith and the doctrine of Jesus Christ have been perverted and compromised over the centuries. In the past, God's people integrated and mixed with other cultures and ethnic groups. This resulted in the introduction of pagan religious beliefs and worship into the Christian faith and religion and way of life. Moreover, that has been the plan of Satan for centuries.

Weaken the people of God to the point that they become weak, passive, and ineffective. So when you speak the word of God, you don't declare it with power and authority. The reason is because we are living a compromised life in God. Because of the way we have been taught, this is the way we are being indoctrinated, to see God in a box, tell Him what you want, and what you need, and He gives it to you.

We don't see God for Who He is, the all-powerful, almighty, sovereign God and as a consequence, that is why we suffer failures upon failures.

God wants us healed, delivered, and set free. He wants us to live a life of victory, walking with confidence by claiming healing, restoration, riches, and favor with God and man.

When you look around, you will see so many of God's people living in poverty and lack, isolated from the truth, and from love. So many of God's people walking around bruised and beaten up by the devil, how can this be?

If we serve a great and mighty God, the all-sufficient God and King, the Creator of all things, why should the children of God be walking around in bondage? We were born in sin and shaped in iniquity, and it has caused so many problems for us as a people. For us to break away from out of these unfortunate situations, we must reform our lives and recondition our minds.

Walk by faith is a complete spiritual revolution, that must take place with us, through us, and within us, and it is a serious determination.

The enemy will attack us hard and be aggressive, try to dismantle our faith and to destroy the relationship you have with your God. So if you don't have the Word of God to stand in your faith, the pushback will always seem that Satan is winning the war against us.

If only we could look through the eyes of God to see His love and affection that He has for His people. The Word of God makes it very clear that through His love, we are more than conquerors through Him who loved us.

Breaking chains over our lives may sound foolish, but it is necessary and real. God revealed this to me from praying for someone with a problematic teenage daughter.

From the beginning of life from conception in the womb as a baby, and through our childhood to teenage years and finally into adulthood, any words spoken over the life of the child by our parents, whether positive or negative, will affect them in the future. The life of a person begins at the moment of conception, that's when the spirit of the child is birthed.

Seventy percent of human life occurs within the womb, so we are living thirty percent outside the womb. It may seem unreal, but it is true. Seventy percent of a person's life occurs within the womb.

The head, the body, the arms, hands, legs, heart, kidneys, lungs, liver and all other body parts all develop and begin to function in the womb. Conscious awareness begins and becomes active in the womb. After birth, we learn, grow and adapt to our environment, culture and beliefs, and everything else formed from within your mother's womb. Human life begins at conception, the spirit of the child comes from the loins of the man in his sperms.

The interaction between the father and mother while the baby is in the womb can affect the development and welfare of the child.

After a child is born, the type of nurturing the child receives until the child becomes a teenager accounts for twenty percent of life experiences.

Ten percent of our life experiences comes when we are adults. Most of the time, things that are happening in our lives today start from within the womb. The experience you have as an adult, the abilities that you have as an adult, comes from when we were nurtured as a baby, and growing up in the tender age of a child, will determine your successes or failures.

The Word of God says train a child in the way he should go, and when he is old, he will not depart from it (Proverbs 22:6). So our adult life is indeed the outcome of our childhood life experience. Moreover, that is why so many people have so many problems. Their lives were being affected, or should I say, infected as a child.

There is always hope. The hope is in the Lord Jesus Christ, the only one who has the power to break the chains, and that is why Jesus Christ came into this world to create and establish a new world, which is the kingdom of God.

The kingdom of God is the body of Jesus Christ, and He made an example for us by showing us the way to live, to be successful, to live a life free from bondage and control from the devil, who has been given power and authority over us through the fall of Adam.

Satan has no power of himself. He has the authority, and the influence he has is what you give to him. He is powerless unless we surrender our self-will to him which will give him power and authority over us. He will use that authority to control, manipulate and destroy us if we surrender our self-will to him.

In our life experiences today, we are exposed to all kinds of things, and we don't know where they came from or how to deal with these problems. Things begin to revolve around us as we see past mistakes happening in our present daily lives, and the same mistakes get repeated in our tomorrow's life experience.

We see things playing out before us that we don't know how to shake off, it can only be done through the mighty name of Jesus Christ. The problems of the world today will not go away; it will never leave us, but we can take control over them and bring them under control. How can we do this? This is for us to be born again

To be born again is when we hear the Word of God and believe in our heart that Jesus Christ is the Son of God. Confess the Word out of our mouth and acknowledge the Word is true. There is a new life that will be birthed within you. It is to be born again, not of flesh nor blood but the spirit.

To be born again, all the curse and corruption are broken from over our lives because you now have a new experience within you now from Christ. Now we need to walk according to the spirit, not according to the dictates of the flesh. When you start walking according to the flesh, the old problems and curse will spring back to life. The scars of your past will come back from your childhood, even from in the womb, and will reappear in the present. The Word of God said, "With lack of knowledge, God's people perish."

We have a lot of good God-loving Christians perishing, who sincerely don't know as they are indoctrinated by false religion. False teaching only creates more bondage in the life of the afflicted and create problems for the ones already delivered.

Breaking chains only operates through the power of the Holy Spirit by repentance, confession, and casting out the evil associated with the problem.

Although evil spirit cannot possess, control to afflict a person's spirit because the man's spirit is created in the image and likeness of God, evil spirits can undoubtedly possess the human body to control, afflict, torment, and destroy the host body.

So evil spirit must be cast out of the flesh, and when it goes from your body, something else must replace it, and it is a fruit of the Holy Spirit. If you have not the fruit of the Holy Spirit, there is something else in control of you that will oppress, frustrate, and torment you and steal your joy and peace. When you develop temperance, love, patience with self-control, the fruit of God is manifest within you.

If there is no fruit, something else is in control!

If the law of the flesh governs you, that means you are administered by and under demonic control. We should be under the guidance of the law of the Spirit of life, and in so doing, this is the only way you can have victory.

"When the enemy shall come in like a flood, the Spirit of the LORD shall lift a standard against him." We see in our day-to-day lives God's people suffering in pain, being shackled, and walking around in bondage, failures, hurt, and pain. We are saying to ourselves, how can these things be? The answer is, we are not living the laws of the spirit, not living according to the truth, which is the Word of God. We are malnourished of knowledge, wisdom, and understanding of God, indoctrinated by false religious beliefs, living and operating among unsaved people.

If you are a Christian living with and operating among unsaved people, you cannot walk in the fullness of God's anointing. If you must be among unsaved people, you must be living and practicing the Word of God that others can read the living word of God in you. True Christians will be proven in their speech, actions, and behaviors in a social atmosphere. Living with unsaved people, if the Word of God is not being played out in your life, you will adapt to their lifestyle.

It will weaken you spiritually, and the carnal man will spring to life. That man that has been conceived in the womb and groomed by a parent who never showed love or care, will curse and beat upon you, because you were never dedicated to Jesus Christ as a baby. If a child is not dedicated, who will lay claim to the soul of the child? A child must be devoted to the Lord at an early stage for God to be responsible for that child.

What do we see in the world today? So many kids are in rebellion. So many kids are being indoctrinated and be sure, when they become adults, these actions will be even worse than their life as a kid because they're now going to live their 70 percent, and their 20 percent, in their 10 percent. The only thing that can bring about a total radical change is to destroy the 100 percent.

Destroying the hundred percent is when you are born again in Christ. "Therefore if any man is in Christ, he is a new creature: old things passed away; behold, all things have become new" (2 Corinthians 5:17). With that hundred percent destroyed, a new man has given birth, and the Bible says, "Know ye not, that so many of us as were baptized into Jesus Christ, were baptized into his death?"

> Therefore we are buried with him by baptism into death: that like as Christ was raised from the dead by the glory of the Father, even so, we also should walk in newness of life and given a new name.

We are now the sons and daughters of God, filled with His Holy Spirit, living with a purpose. We are now royalty, in the kingdom of God a royal priest, and engrafted into the olive branch of the Lord, sons and daughters of God, no longer an ordinary people but extraordinary people.

That is what happens when you become a new creation in Christ. That is what breaks the chains that holds us hostage; that, when you are about to see victory in your life, you are being pulled back like a dog that has been chained up.

You put food in front of him; he runs towards the food and before he reaches it, the chain restrains him. In a similar manner, you see your dreams, aspirations, and the potential for greatness at your fingertips; but for some unknown reason, it just cannot be achieved.

You have that beauty and personality to become a great wife or husband, but every relationship is a broken one because something keeps yanking on that chain that holds you hostage.

The moment it seems that you are about to have a breakthrough, you're pulled back from that opportunity of getting that great job. As you were about to walk in it, you are pulled back. As you're about to walk in your healing and restoration, as soon as it's about to happen, you are pulled back. You see everything before you and the potential of having it—that beautiful car, a beautiful house, and excellent life—all becomes so difficult to obtain. You have the potential but you are unable to succeed in life.

That is the chain the enemy has placed upon us!

Praise the Lord. Now that you have achieved all that you have dreamed and hoped for, you are now faced with new challenges, a mountain of obstacles and problems to keep you from maintaining that which you have labored so hard to accomplish.

Because we are in the flesh, controlled by evil forces of darkness that we were born and raised with, we need to be born again to receive the overcoming power of the Holy Spirit's anointing, wisdom, knowledge and understanding with counsel and might. The Spirit of Might gives you the unknown ability to go beyond your ability to accomplish anything. "I can do all things through Christ which strengthened me" (Philippians 4:13).

> For with God nothing shall be impossible.
> (Luke 1:37)

When we are born again, we are able to walk in the power and authority of the Holy Spirit to break the chains that hold us hostage and in bondage. As children of God, seeing those things playing out in our lives that has happened yesteryear in our today and shaping up to happen in our tomorrow will repeat itself. We need to go to the cross, lay our burden down, put it all before God, and take authority. Command those evil things to leave now in the name of Jesus Christ.

If there is anything in your life, items or images associated with evil, throw it out. Purge yourself and your home. Then you are able to walk in the power of God. Don't compromise your faith. Walk in integrity. Healing may seem very hard, but it is easy. What makes it hard is the evil and wicked opposition orchestrated against you.

When you begin to clear the webs and clouds, break down the walls, you will be able to see all these obstacles, all that it was.

The barriers are obstacles that made it difficult to realize our goals and dreams. All we need to do is break the chains in our lives, and the chain could be poverty, lack, hurt, pain, sorrow, unforgiveness, curses pronounced over our lives, even from our parents, not able to forgive yourself from past mistakes and failures.

We need to let God within our hearts. The battle is already won through the power of the blood. Only through His power can we break the chains. His power can break any chains. We need to exercise that power by the Word of God in Jesus' name.

Chapter 12

And Suddenly! The Damascus-Road Experience

Each of us have our own Damascus Road. We have that zeal to do great things when everything feels right, seems reasonable, real, and truthful. Believing in ourselves with a firm conviction, and with that same conviction, thinking that what we are doing is so right, we feel empowered in doing and advancing to achieve those goals. We believe with all our heart that this is what is necessary for the moment to get rich and become great; this is a blessing of God.

Let's take a look at a prominent figure in the Word of God. Paul, formerly known as Saul, will illustrate how we can be led by our conviction in what we are doing to be right when in God's sight, it is not divinely ordained.

Saul had a zeal. He genuinely believed that persecuting Christians for their faith was the right thing to do. He had this conviction that Christians were blaspheming God in this newly birthed religion, and putting these people to death at all costs was the right thing for him to do, a commission by God for him to carry out.

Many of us have a similar strong zeal in pursuit of our dreams and our belief.

We say to ourselves, "We need to get things done. I have a strong belief. I know this is right." Saul had a similar conviction.

In Acts chapter 9 verse 1, it reads, "And Saul yet breathing out threatening and slaughter against the disciples of the Lord, went unto the high priest, and desired of him letters to Damascus to the synagogues, that if he found any of this way, whether they were men or women, he might bring them bound unto Jerusalem."

Saul had this conviction: he had this strong belief that what he was doing was right.

So as he journeyed, he came near Damascus, and suddenly there shone around him a light from heaven. He came near Damascus to fulfill his purpose, dreams, and belief with much zeal. How many of us, in pursuing our goals and visions, come so near to bringing it to pass, and in a moment, everything changes? Something happens to put you on a different path. At that point, we feel so discouraged, angry, filled with disappointment and disbelief.

Saul traveled all the way from Jerusalem to Damascus and had come so close to accomplishing and fulfilling his dreams and desires with intense zeal. Then the unexpected "and suddenly" occurred.

In our life, we have these types of "and suddenly"! Unexpected experiences. It comes at a time when everything seems right. It comes in a time when it seems we can fulfill our dreams. The "and suddenly!" happens and changes the entire plan or destiny of our life.

Never expecting disappointments to show up, we want to continue as planned. All our goals, dreams, and aspirations for success, relationship and travel plans, come to a halt.

However, when the "and suddenly" shows up, it brings pain, hurt, humiliation, shame. The hopelessness that will break our stride breaks our faith, have us question the reason behind all that we are trying to do and accomplish. The "and suddenly" is when God shows up to stop us from hurting ourselves; it comes when we are walking against the will of God.

Because we desire not to know the will of God for our life, we want to move on and accomplish something we wish, no longer what God desires but to achieve our set goals. It's like saying, "Lord, my will be done, not yours." But what we should be saying is, "Lord, let your will be done, not mine." So we want God to approve the assignment that we may be on, approve the journey, because we don't have any patience. We want to fit God in a box, and He must answer to our request!

There shines around him a light from heaven. There are times when we are on a path. We believe it will guarantee success, and suddenly something shows up! Like a mirror, a reflection of our life. We see our mistakes, our failures, because the light of God has come to expose our hidden flaws and buried secrets; the pains, anger, and unforgiveness that we have been living with and sheltered, hiding in our career and likable personalities and flawless behavior and emotions.

We are blinded by our zeal and determination with poor judgment and selfish ambitions to accomplish the journey. Something happened. We were able to see ourselves. The light of God shines in our heart, exposing that dark hidden secret by our conscience, making known to us the reality of our vain pursuit. "And he fell to the earth, and heard a voice."

The Bible talks about seeds. Unless a seed is sown into the ground, it will not be able to bring forth life and break out of the core. The life of the tree is inside the seed.

Some of us need to fall to ground level to establish a new beginning before God in brokenness, that we can see our true self, look at our flaws and see clearly the path was the wrong path. So falling to the ground helps us break from the web of denial and come to terms and accept our true self. Living a life of pretense with no money, no friends or spiritual support will make you frustrated, and tormented with a self-driven ego.

So falling to the ground enables you to see clearly and understand that there is something far much greater than chasing after false hope, false peace, and there is more to life by accepting Jesus Christ as Lord and Savior.

Falling is not a bad thing; it sometimes wakes us up to a destructive path we may be traveling. However, your determination getting up is when you know and understand the reason for the fall. A seed must fall to the earth before it can bring forth existence. Life is in the seed; all the harvest is in the grains. So Saul had to drop to the earth to hear the voice of God for the Holy Spirit imparted in his being.

When we are full of zeal, energy, strength, self-righteousness, thinking that we are so righteous, honorable, and perfect, we must fall to wake up to be broken to hear the voice of God. Also, many of us will never hear God until we make mistakes, then rebuked or chastised for our selfishness, arrogance, and pride. When we fall, the voice will be heard clearly, "Saul, Saul, why persecute thou me?" That was strange to Saul because Saul believed he was on a mission from God. He was doing what God required him to do: to destroy these people whom he considered to be blaspheming against God in this new faith.

Many believers are on a journey, full of zeal, and the path that they are on is a wrong path. Their enthusiasm and misguided zeal will not accomplish anything until they all come to realize themselves they must be able to hear the voice of God.

Saul heard the voice, "Why persecute thou me?" And he said, "Who are thou, Lord!" So the Lord said, "I am Jesus, whom thou persecuted."

He was full of zeal for God, but did not know and understand the will of God and desired purpose for his life. So without God's guidance for the mission, he was on a dark road, a mysterious journey.

Many people are on a mission for God, but they don't have a relationship with Him. So they are doing something for someone whom they know not of, and that can be very complicated. You're on assignment, and you don't know who assigned the task.

You have no relationship and that means you can easily be fooled, be easily tricked, into believing a lie, and you have false hope and false zeal because the source is wrong. But if the source is wrong, everything else will be wrong.

The Damascus Road in our life is necessary. Falling is also essential, and sometimes the "and suddenly"! That brings about the fall that is necessary to wake us up from this selfish zeal and appetite.

Many of us have experienced the "and suddenly." Things happen, and it changes your life. When you get that phone call or message that hurts you deeply because you were not expecting bad news, you feel like something good has been ripped out of you. It was not supposed to happen that way. You had your life perfectly planned out and this terrible thing happened and changed everything from good to bad to worse.

This was never part of the plan, you did not expect this nightmare to happen, and suddenly, this nightmarish experience caused us to see the light and to hear the voice.

I am Jesus whom thou persecuted; it is hard for thee to kick against the pricks.

You are on a zeal for God, but the enthusiasm is an artificial zeal. What is supposed to feel right for you is wrong. What is to be true is now an error, and you are kicking again something that you should be supporting, and you have the conviction of doing just that.

You cannot bring about change in a person who does not believe what they are doing is wrong and they have a firm conviction that their actions are right and just. Unless this person encounters the "And Suddenly" experience, falls to the ground and hears the voice, they would always be on that path, and sometimes not many people listen to the voice. Not many people when they fall to the ground hear the voice, and you say to yourself, why?

God loves when you are direct and positive concerning what you believe in. With that motion, in that setting, He can reveal Himself; but if you're not on the path of a journey, and you have no zeal for something, you will never find a zeal for God.

A person who is very passive, lukewarm, will never find the zeal for God because they have no enthusiasm for anything. A person who cannot make up their mind for something, how can they make up their mind to serve God?

So when you go out there making a mistake, God loves a person who will make a mistake because they are trying to accomplish something, and errors is the most excellent teacher for wisdom. Experience teaches wisdom.

Moreover, he was trembling and astonished and said, "Lord, what wilt thou have me to do? And the Lord said unto him, Arise, and go into the city, and it shall have told thee what thou must do." When we have a new experience that shakes us to the core, and suddenly experience, we will always find ourselves trembling, find ourselves astonished.

If you have an experience, that "and suddenly" experience, and you're not trembling and astonished, it has not shaken you to the core. Sometimes we experience some things, a sudden shock. We get nervous, having no control over the emotions that causes us to tremble in fear and astonishment. At that point, so many things begin to go through our thought process, the what-ifs? Thoughts start to go through our mind because of "the and suddenly" experience.

That light that shines in our understanding causes us to see so many things, both positive and the negative all at once, and life flashes before us. Then we start to weigh the circumstances, what if the outcome was like this or that way? That is the moment that we would hear the voice, that is when God is derailing us from our own purpose.

And the Lord said unto him, "Arise, and go into the street which is called Straight, and inquire in the house of Judas for one called Saul, of Tarsus: for, behold, he prayed."

Then comes our instructions, what needs to be done because when you find yourself in a situation, the "and suddenly moment," and you are on the ground, and you hear the voice, you desire specific instructions. You also want understanding and counsel; that's why the Damascus Road experience is always necessary.

When you're full of zeal and hopes and on the wrong path, you would undoubtedly be awakened by God.

And the men which journeyed with him stood speechless because they heard the voice but could see no man speaking.

When you're on the Damascus Road and have the Damascus Road experience that suddenly occurs, people around you will never know what's happening to you. They may think they know, but they never know because this is something that is truly deep, concerning you and associated with God.

There is always a reason for everything; the reason why God will take you down, and some of these reasons, if not all these reasons, usually are personal between you and God.

Because you alone underwent an experience that nobody else knows about, you alone know the reasons for your zeal and desires, and when things happen, people don't understand, but you understand the reason for the situation happening in your life.

You may choose to ignore or suppresses it, but it will never go away. It will always be present. It's still good to face up to the things that are bothering you and not suppress your concerns.

Because suppressing it would always do us wrong, and the devil loves secrets. He should know your secrets, but nobody else should know he would use what he considers a secret to manipulate and try to destroy you.

Chapter 13

Blind Faith, Hopeless Ambitions

It Is What It Is!

We are seeing things breaking apart by the minute and hourly, things are getting out of control, and we have to realize and understand that the things that seem out of control are indeed under God's control. People who seem to be out of control are living their destiny. They are fulfilling something that needs to happen. If people don't get crazy, there is no need for mental institutions, treatment by professionals, brain surgeons for the sick with brain disorders. There is no need for hospitals, doctors, nurses, and average workers.

If you don't have a problem with your plumbing, there is no need for a plumber, no stuff to throw out, no need for a garbage collector. This is a cycle. This is a process the world goes through. Despite how chaotic it may seem, everything has its rightful place, and God permits every sequence of events to happen.

> In whom also we have obtained an inheritance, being predestinated according to the purpose of him who worketh all things after the counsel of his own will. (Ephesians 1:11)

We are living in a perfect world according to God's standard, but in our eyes, it is imperfect, dangerous or out of control, awaiting the destruction and annihilation of life. However, that's what makes it perfect because it's an ongoing cycle to fulfill God's purpose.

It goes around, and for years and centuries, man has been having the same problems, and it doesn't change the sun from shining, the rain from falling. It doesn't change anything. Man dies, babies are born—the same cycle, recycled all over again.

The same problems: mountain of issues. There is no end in sight for the problems. However, with your problems, it's somebody else's solution. That's why we have issues because when the problem is solved, it fixes the situation for somebody else.

Great men of faith suffered and died through persecution from evil men for us today to be the beneficiary of the Word of God explained to us directly and understandably. Even though the world is chaotic, it is a perfect place because everything is appropriate according to a cycle. You will know there is a severe problem when there is no longer any sunlight and there is no rainfall.

Nature has a way to cleanse herself. Forest fires are nature's way of cleansing the earth's surface. After a period of time, the trees and the grass begin to grow back. The burned trees, bushes and grass become a part of the soil as a rich layer of fertilizer which promotes a healthier growth for the trees and grass that provides food and shelter for animals. It's all a cycle, so when man disturbs nature, they will find themselves chewed up and spat out because it was meant to be that way. We try to change so many things, and in the course of doing so, the very thing automatically changes us.

So we are fighting against a law, the law of nature. We are fighting against an act of truth, which is an act of God, for what is very real and does exist—*truth*.

When we begin to push back against the law of truth, we find ourselves oppressed, frustrated, and angry. Know the truth, and the truth is what will set us free to accept life for what it is and believe that we have a God, the Creator, the mighty, the sovereign God and King. He is in control of all things, living and the dead.

Many people fail to accept the truth for what it is, and that's what causes pressure, frustration, and worry. You see a problem over there, you would want the issues fixed, but you don't have the power to repair it, so what you do? Worry! Then you start doing things to make something happen, but the more you try to change it, the more it remains the same or becomes much worse, worse than where it was before you got started.

What happens next? You start to get anxious, begin to develop and entertain doubt, low self-esteem, and discouragement, thinking to yourself, "I am not capable of achieving, doing, and getting anything right."

However, the truth is that thing is way beyond you, so whatsoever you can't fix, leave it alone. It will certainly hurt and destroy you in the process, and the original state remains the same.

Complaining about the heat from the sun and feeling miserable is a waste of time especially when you can't control the temperature of the sun. It's far easier to find a shaded spot and get out of the heat. It's that simple and easy. Too often, people like to complain about everything and instead of looking for solutions, they create more problems. They feel more comfortable in a constant state of misery and negativity. Quit murmuring and complaining! It doesn't change anything except to make the situation more stressful, bothersome and painful.

Life was meant to be easy, but we make it complicated and complex because we cannot accept what we see before us, so we try to make it into something else other than what it was meant to be. Moreover, that is our biggest problem. We become unhappy and miserable; we see something blue and wish it was red. When the blue cannot change to red, we then pour all kinds of different colors over it to change it so we can be convinced how we view it. But the fact is, changing something is not the solution. We are the ones that need to change.

We can live a lie and deceive ourselves that what is in front of us is not real, but we cannot change the facts of what is real to be unreal. So many people try to live a lie and live in denial, hoping that to believe otherwise, it will change or go away, but it will not be so.

Some things that exist, we cannot change. Why allow it to affect us? We must accept it for what it is, and if we are going to do something for change, start do something about your mind-set to make a change concerning your perspective.

However, you cannot change it because the elements of itself need to change without you being able to turn it.

Many people desire to change other people to become something they are not, but it will never happen unless the person is willing to accept change. So we see the potential for other people, but the person you see the potential for, don't see it in themselves. What can you do? You only can encourage such a one to believe their hidden potential by trying to convince and supporting them. You cannot change anyone to live their potential; it will not happen. They will have to come to terms with themselves to see things your way.

At times, we carry blind imagination, seeing things for what it can become and want to live it as though it can be. When proven not to be so, we then create images in our mind, looking at the situation, not seeing the situation for what it is but understanding the situation for what it could be, so we accept the "could be" when the situation is *what it is*! That could be called blind faith.

Faith is the substance of things hoped for, the evidence of things not seen. However, having faith in the person in whom you believe in, must be God-inspired, God driven, and God motivated. Believing in something without belief in God is blind faith.

So we are seeing something that doesn't exist, hoping and believing that it can come to pass, or if it exists, when it does not. Many people are living in denial, with false hopes, dreams and unrestrained self-confidence, unable to believe the truth and accept it for what it is.

It can be very complicated when it has not been determined by faith in God. We are not to accept sicknesses, or live with it, because illnesses are influenced by evil. This has to do with things that are unseen and beyond us, but with a clear understanding of your faith in God the chains can be broken.

To have the power to bring about change, such as stopping the sun from shining, or the rain from falling, is beyond our power, and we cannot make any changes concerning that matter. Such is nature. But with sickness, we can do something about it, like changing our eating habits, doing exercises, getting medical attention, changing attitudes, relationships, and changing our personal environment.

However, some things can never change in the law of nature; that is something we don't have the power to do, even when we are believing and praying to God for it. God will not go against His laws because we complain about it. So we must abide in the laws of God and recognize it for what it is and have respect for it. When it rains, we use an umbrella or raincoat to keep ourselves dry. We need not live a lie, live truth, see a thing for what it is, and deal with it in the way it presents itself to be.

We don't want to make a great deal out of something when it is nothing. Coming to terms with our lives allow us to deal with the most challenging situations we will face in our lives. Nothing in and of itself is hard. The Bible says, "There is nothing new upon the face of the earth, everything that we lived; was already lived by somebody before us." The difficulties we face, someone before us faced similar or even worse troubles.

All we need to do is to train our mind, educate our attitude, by teaching ourselves to live the word of God that we can discern truth from error.

Living in and adhering to the Word of God is relevant and essential to fulfill godly wisdom and power for success and prosperity.

> The children of Issachar, which were men that
> understood the times, to know what Israel ought
> to do. (1 Chronicles 12:32, KJV)

When we are going into a war, it is good to have people who can understand the times, how to wage war, how to fight a war, how to win the battle, how to plan to be strategic with the necessary tools and equipment to war.

With an understanding of the enemy tactics we are about to face, if we don't know and understand our enemy, we will be defeated.

Many people don't like to talk about the devil. Don't go there! Don't talk about the devil because! Why talk about the devil? Talk about positive things. Talk about God.

We are in a continuous warfare, a warfare that never ceases, a warfare that has been going on long before us, and is still being waged today. Many people have died during this continuing warfare, and many more people will die for others to live during this warfare. We are in an active state of war against the enemy and the forces of darkness regardless of whether you choose to believe it or not.

The only way we can defeat the enemy, the devil, Satan the dragon, is to understand the enemy. Satan is always at work, and we cannot wish that the devil doesn't exist and think that things will change if only we have a different mindset. Incredible as it sounds, there are many Christians who don't believe that the devil exists. He is real and if you continue to deny his existence, he has succeeded in deceiving you.

We are up against a master plan of the devil to derail us, trying to stop and destroy the people of God. Satan is like a roaring lion seeking whom he may devour, and when he tries to deceive us, it is with lies.

The devil wants to keep us in our comfort zone, blaming God for every bad thing that happens while keeping us in the dark that he is the one working hard to derail us from God's purpose. He wants us to live a passive, ineffective life in our decision-making, walking in confusion, and seeing others as the problem, so when the blame game comes around to blame someone, it's never your fault, it's always someone else at fault.

Many times, people make a foolish choice, sincerely believing it is the right thing to do, and that doesn't make them guilty, but it opens doors for demonic attacks based upon the lack of knowledge, guidance, and direction.

Calling it an excuse is not an escape route to obtain a different result. What has been done can never be undone. Fix the problem by making the necessary repairs before it becomes an exhibition for failures and embarrassment.

Chapter 14

Breaking Away from Yesterday's Fears into Today's Success

*P**rophetic word from God: Moses, now dead, represents our past life living in this shameful world in sin. Joshua represents the calling of God to the church, to face up to the challenges of the faith.*

Moses, My Servant Is Dead

Joshua Chapter 1. God did not speak with Joshua until Moses was dead. Now that Moses is dead, the mantle of God needed to pass down to the next in line. No matter how anointed we are, no matter how gifted we are, God does things in order.

God recognizes spiritual authority. He will never speak to someone lesser in authority when the one superior in authority is still alive. He will only speak to the person who is superior in authority because God is a God of order.

Moses is dead! And that is what God is saying to Joshua, "Moses is now dead!" What is God saying here? There are some things in life that we must let go when it's time to move on.

There are some things we cherish that are important in our lives: an old friendship, an old job, our old lifestyle. We must accept that all these important things in our lives are forever gone in order to transition ourselves to accept change.

God said to Joshua, "Joshua, Moses is now dead!" Sometimes some things have to be riveted. Sometimes some things have to be spoken out clearly and loudly so that we are able to understand the intent of the spoken words to make change.

There are times when we are looking at something but not fully focusing our attention on it. If we can see it for what it truly represents, our view and understanding would be different in order to facilitate a change in perspective.

Come On! Move On! Stop Whining!

> Moses my servant is dead. Now therefore arise,
> go over this Jordan, you and all these people, into
> the land which I am giving to them, to the people
> of Israel. (Joshua 1:2)

Now God is saying, "Arise, come on! Move on! Stop mourning! Stop looking down on yourself, stop underestimating your abilities. Recognize that you have the power to lead and do great things. Why live in the shadow of Moses because he is now dead?"

He was the one who held you in high esteem, taught you, and guided you. He allowed you to remain relevant in your comfort zone. But now things have changed because the image of Moses you held in high esteem is no longer relevant.

The wall that you have been hiding behind, that image of the person that you have been striving to be and not allowing your true self to shine, is now dead! It is time to come in from the shadows, step into the light, step up and do something different. You are no longer a follower; you are now the leader. You now have a great responsibility, and you must live it, accept it, and believe it because Moses is now dead.

Too often many of us hold on to dead things hoping that they will spring to life. So many of us are living a lie, living in deception, believing in something that doesn't exist, if only it could be like a fairy tale. But it is the here and now, and things have changed.

How many of us keep holding on, believing that we can make something out of the thing that is now gone? There is nothing in it. It is time to move on, time to forget the losses, time to bury Moses.

Bury the pain, bury the hurt, bury the lies and deceit. Bury that old relationship and move on from the Moses of your past who used to make a difference, but not anymore.

The sense of security is now gone. Moses was everything that we needed, everything that we desired. Now things have changed because the now dead Moses is of the past and must now be put to rest. If we continue to live as though Moses is alive, we will experience dead hope, dried-up experiences, a life of dormancy with no blessing. It's time to move on and take up the mantle of faith and exercise it.

> Every place that the sole of your foot shall tread upon, that have I given unto you, as I said unto Moses.

God is now making a declaration onto Joshua: he is no longer an understudy and a servant of Moses. Joshua must now step into the limelight; he must be able to make sound judgments to lead the people according to the Word of God, and that's a big responsibility.

There are times in life when serious decisions must be made to take responsibility, to stop procrastinating, to recognize that things are not the same and do things differently.

We should not shape our lives adversely; the same thing will not work going through the transitions of life. Moses's way of doing things will not work the same; we must adjust our life to accommodate the change. The same old things will not work in a new environment. With new counsel and a new leader to guide the people, old things will not work; therefore, we must be willing to adapt to new changes.

> There shall not any man be able to stand before thee all the days of thy life: as I was with Moses, so I will be with thee: I will not fail thee, nor forsake thee.

Sometimes we need that reassurance from families and friends even though we believe but are sincerely struggling with our faith. Because there is not that driving force behind us to motivate and encourage us to walk that path.

No matter how risky it may become, it is necessary and good to have people to whom you can count on, to speak life into your spirit to cope with the difficult situations. No complainers, no murmurers, no doubters to speak negatives. We need just that one person to stand in agreement with us.

God was speaking and encouraging Joshua to have a new mindset, a new way of thinking, to take a different approach rather than the old and familiar way he used to govern himself. You are no longer a servant but a leader; your approach must be different. Your attitude must be discreet. The way you perceive things must be different. When you dress, it must be different; old things will not work with the new.

The Moses lifestyle is dead. The way you walk and talk must be different because people are now looking to you for guidance or encouragement. So what you used to do under the old Moses system will not work anymore. There is no Moses to guide and strengthen you when things become very hard and difficult in your life.

In our faith, we cannot adapt to or continue the same path we used when we were unsaved. Things have to change; things must turn around. That Moses era is past, and now you're in a different era in your life. Strong and correct decisions must be made without getting entangled and trapped in a web by becoming enslaved to other people's burdens, problems, and confusing situations. Not knowing what to do to escape sinful circumstances, we find ourselves living lies, not able to see the truth, nor crying out to God in fear and brokenness.

Sometimes we need to reassure ourselves by reading the Word of God. We must declare by faith, "We can do all things through Christ who strengthens me" because that lifestyle you lived in the world is now dead.

With Joshua, now given the responsibility to lead the children of Israel into the Promised Land, he must be responsible, to walk by the leading and fruit of the Holy Spirit, being empowered by God; so it is with our faith in Jesus Christ.

> There shall not any man be able to stand before thee all the days of thy life: as I was with Moses, so I will be with thee: I will not fail thee, nor forsake thee.

With all these words coming from God, if we don't believe or accept the word for what it is, it means nothing. God said to Joshua, "I will stand with thee. So I was with Moses, I'm also with you; I will not fail you; I will not forsake you." God says what He means and means what He says. God has said these same words to many of us multiple times, yet we still have not come to the fullness in accepting or appreciating it so that we will see the results.

Here, God is saying to Joshua, "Be strong and of good courage." That is very important because how can God say to someone who is weak, "Be strong!"? How can you tell someone who is fearful not to worry, to be courageous? To be strong and of good courage, you must believe God and take Him at His word.

If you cannot believe God and take him at his word, nothing that God says will matter. This is because the devil will always be working against you in an attempt to disrupt your faith in God.

God knew what Joshua was about to face: temptations from close friends and family members. People who were skeptics wanted to break his spirit, his zeal, and drive. This was no different than from a serpent's or hyena's subtle and deceptive schemes, trying to break your spirit and drive. It would be a serious weakness on your path to trust, believe, or depend on these people. Being lovers of themselves, boastful, proud, and detractors of the faith, what state will you be in when all these things begin to come up against you?

So many things are happening in our life, and God is saying to Joshua, "Be strong and of good courage, for unto these people you will decide for an inheritance, as I promised your fathers to give them."

God reassured Joshua by saying, "Be so strong and courageous," which was very important. Moses was dead; the mantle was now given unto Joshua. No more would he be able to hide in the shadow of Moses. Now he had people to shepherd into their deliverance and do what Moses had done and even more. God was saying to Joshua, "Be strong be of good courage, only be strong and courageous." If you do that, God will be able to do the rest because you are trusting in God for the impossible, and whenever you start to waver and doubt, God is saying, "Only be strong and courageous."

You're confronting your Goliath; you know that you don't have the ability to take him down. God will take down the Goliath on your behalf. You only need to be strong in order to stand before the Goliath. If you are unable to stand before him, you cannot see the hands of God working on your behalf. If there is no Goliath, there is no hands of God.

So God is saying, "Joshua, be strong and very courageous." God is not asking Joshua for anything here, not asking him to be brilliant, not asking if he is capable. He's not asking for his qualification. All He is saying, is "Just only be thou strong and courageous!"

The enemy is always trying to wear us down, pushing us against the wall to let us feel hopeless. That's all the enemy wants to do: break our stride, have us to doubt and be insecure, and to have so many questions with very few answers.

God is saying to Joshua, "Just be strong and trust the Lord," even when it doesn't seem to be possible, even when it doesn't feel right.

You have an unsaved husband or wife. Because of his or her behavior, it doesn't seem possible that they will ever accept change, or the day will never arrive for them to accept the Lord as Savior. Problems at the workplace, unending stress and pressure, feeling all types of pains in my body, doubtful and oppressive feeling, whispers of thoughts going through my mind, *You can't make it.*

God knows all these negatives. He knows what's going on in the heart of Joshua. When does the reality hit home? When does the reality truly confront Joshua? It's when he doesn't see Moses in the morning but instead sees the rebellious people who will challenge his authority.

"So you think you are Moses?" Satan will send people to undermine your authority and abilities by trying to weaken your capability. God knows. He is listening to your pains and frustrations and will answer your cry to comfort, strengthen, and deliver you from evil men who will undermine your character, curse at you, try to diminish who you are and what you stand for. But God is saying to Joshua just only be so strong and very courageous. It's not that Joshua is courageous. God is speaking life into Joshua's spirit, to be courageous, and He will do great things on his behalf.

Only be thou strong and courageous and observe to do all according to all the law. Being strong and courageous enables you to observe and do according to all the laws. Many people are unable to find the courage to fight, to stand up to their adversaries, because they are demotivated with zero zeal or fire in them to do anything. So therefore, God is saying, "Be strong and be very courageous," which enables you to observe.

When you are courageous, you can observe. A weak and fearful person cannot observe because they are looking out for themselves. But they who are strong and courageous find methods and ways of doing things and make it happen.

Being courageous and being strong enables you to observe, to do according to the law, and follow instruction. If you are aware, you will find strength in courage. By being strong, you will not be intimidated by the things that are around you.

> Only be thou strong and very courageous, that thou mayest observe to do according to all the law, which Moses my servant commanded thee: turn not from it to the right hand or to the left, that thou mayest prosper whithersoever thou goes.

There is a key to prosperity, a key to your benefits to shut doors to poverty and open doors to wealth and greatness. We need to take courage and be strong in order to observe and to do according to all the laws of God. It's important that you turn neither to the right nor to the left.

Just like Peter beckoned to Jesus and asked, "Can I come?" Jesus said, "Come," and Peter jumped out of the boat and began to walk on the water to the Lord. Then there was a tempest in the oceans. Peter took his eyes from the Lord for a moment to gaze, and he began to sink. He cried out to the Lord for help! Jesus took him by the hands, pulling him out of the water and into the boat. Jesus said to Peter, "At what moment had you doubted?"

What caused Peter to doubt? The moment Peter took his eyes from the Lord, he was distracted. What happened? He began to sink. What does this mean to us? We are strongly encouraged to observe and do according to the law by not turning to the left nor to right. Stay focused on the prize!

When you keep your eyes focused, it enables you to prosper everywhere you go. You cannot be easily fooled, tricked, or be distracted or manipulated. You won't be fearful but have courage and strength. To know and keep the law and to observe according to everything, do matters in our Christian walk. There are so much failures in our Christian journey because we lose heart being distracted. Distraction brings about failures.

This book of the law must not depart from your mouth because it is showing Joshua the way to prosperity, the way to overcome the enemy, how to have victories.

There are some fundamentals necessary to have victory. God is saying to Joshua, "Be thou courageous; be thou strong in order that you can observe. Don't be distracted by turning to the left or to the right. In so doing, you will prosper everywhere you go."

You have to come to terms with yourself. Bury the Moses of your past, the old way of thinking, the old life, old habits. Stop cheating and telling lies. Bury your fears, unforgiveness, resentment. Take on the attributes of God.

Chapter 15

God Is in Control

We will indeed see problems every day of our lives. We must understand that we are in a battle, a constant warfare, with no referee and it is not a fair fight. The enemy will use every dirty trick to achieve victory. The devil will come up against you, and he thinks of every possible way to defeat you; we must be thinking likewise. We cannot be friends and associate with lovers of wrongdoing. We cannot reason with, or trust the devil. He will make any promise to gain your trust, to get you to sign on the dotted line but beware, he is looking for the first opportunity to destroy you.

> Be sober, be vigilant; because of your adversary the devil, as a roaring lion, walketh about, seeking whom he may devour. (1 Peter 5:8)

The multitude of problems that we face, the many different circumstances that we are in, we must realize that everything happens for a reason. We must face up to that reality! Talking with a friend the other day, he said, "Every man is free to do whatsoever he wants to do because he has free will." However, freedom does come with limitations. We may want to think that we are free, but we are not free as we would want to think or believe. Everything that we do, God knows about it. Even before we think it or act on it, God knows about it.

It's very foolish to believe that God is not in full control of man's destiny and existence. That would mean He is not in control of the world. It is crucial to know, in every action you take, every decision you make, God knows. He knows about the processes you are going through in this life journey.

The processes and experience of life belong to you, and you may choose any which way you want to go, but you will always end with the results that are destined and ordained for your life. God has a blueprint concerning everyone's life. We will be very foolish to believe that man's existence depends upon intellect, abilities, status, beauty, and self-image. However, it's all built upon God's foundational plan, purposes, and pleasure (Ephesians 1:9).

> I call heaven and earth to record this day against you that I have set before you, life and death, blessing and cursing: choose life. (Deuteronomy 30:19)

God is not at some far place not knowing what's happening in our day-to-day life. He is very much involved in our day-to-day activities. He is involved in the choices we make, the decision we take. He is involved in every little details, steps, and aspect of our life, so it would be foolish to believe otherwise.

God is in control! He is in control of our lives; in every action, He is in control. Praise be to God, hallelujah. Praise the Lord.

> As he has received Christ Jesus the Lord, so walk he in him. (Colossians 2:6)

How do you walk in the Lord? You have accepted Christ; walk in Him. The moment we come to Jesus Christ as Lord and Savior, we were baptized or submerged in His life, and there is a way to walk that is in righteousness and holiness and love.

Righteousness is right standing with God, and the Bible says that Jesus is the way, the truth, and the life. So *truth* means to walk in all honesty and in integrity and step by faith because without faith, it is impossible to please God.

We cannot please him with emotions; we can't please Him with our feelings. We only can please Him by believing, by having faith in

Him. So walk in Him, rooted and built top in Him. *Rooted* means you are grounded with a robust and secure foundation in God, which will support your growth because a tree's stand is as strong as the depth of its roots.

So when the challenges and problems come, what determines that you can stand is how much you are rooted in your faith, how rooted you are in a relationship with God. Many times, when bad things start to happen, it's so easy to blame, get angry, and curse at God, not knowing that God is indeed in control and not out of control. Also, sometimes the things that are happening are only a test to see how we will handle the situation.

Are we going to take responsibility for the things that are happening? Alternatively, are we going to blame someone else for the things that have happened?

> Built up and rooted and established in the faith.
> (Colossians 2:7)

It has to do with how you were taught and trained and your understanding put in motion by practicing your belief and being guided and led by the Holy Spirit.

Because things are going to come your way, that's going to test you to see how much you have learned and understood. You cannot know your full potential until it has been challenged or tested. That will determine how rooted and grounded you are in Christ.

How many of us make it a regular practice to be thankful to God for everything, despite failures, despite our hurts, going through our troubled times? How many of us just give God thanks?

Give God thanks! The Bible says that God respects a thankful heart. Enter His gates with thanksgiving and into His courts with praise. When you are approaching the throne of God, thankfulness is very important. It opens the gates unto you for worship and praise, just by being thankful and having a grateful heart. If we don't have a grateful heart, we will have an unthankful heart, and that's not the fruit of God.

It's also important to know that when you are rooted and grounded, built up and established in the faith, it's based upon what you were taught, in the Word of God.

> Beware lets any man spoilt you through philoso-
> phies and vain deceit, after the tradition of men,
> after the rudiments of this world, and not after
> Christ. (Verse 8)

So we can easily be swayed and deceived based on how we were trained and how we learned. That's why we need to go back to the basics to understand the foundation in which to build upon our faith. That's why the Bible talks about being rooted and built upon because if you are not rooted and grounded, it will be easy for you to fall or to sway or to lose hope.

There are so many things out there that can recondition your mind to think thoughts other than that of God, and it will shape things in your mind, and your spirit, as though it is of God. We must be careful about different things out there that has to do with traditions and the involvement of things surrounding this world that has nothing to do with Christ. We must have it in our mind and spirit that God is in control of everything no matter what. God is in control!

The enemy would want you to believe otherwise, and when we see things happening, we want to think that Satan is winning. Because people who are not serving God seem to be the ones who are prospering and given many favors. However, that's not the case.

The goal for God's people is not for earthly possession and great wealth; the goal is to have a place with God in heaven.

The Kingdom of Heaven

The kingdom of heaven is within you: peace, joy, in the Holy Spirit. We are placed temporarily on this earth. So many people possess so many things, yet it seems as if they don't maintain anything.

Because they cannot use the money that they have, the wealth possessed is used to buy freedom and joy with contentment.

They can't be happy because happiness is circumstantial. It comes with a situation at the moment. Take away that situation, what do you have? When the house is gone, the car is gone, the money and wealth are gone, what do you have?

All that person will begin to experience is loneliness, poverty, unhappiness, and misery. Money cannot mend all your problems because you can be in a crowd, and you're lonely. You can have all the wealth and prosperity and still be miserable because it cannot fill that void that requires God.

> For in him dwells all the fullness of the Godhead
> bodily. (Verse 9)

In Christ Jesus, the Son of God, dwells all the Godhead, The Father, The Son, the Holy Spirit. Being complete in Him makes Christ the head of all the Principalities and Powers. However, based on how the devil is operating, you'd want to believe that he is in control when you look on this world, how chaotic it is, and it appears the evil ones are running the show, and God's people are defeated. You want to believe that the principalities and powers are in control. But the Word of God is saying something different here.

If we could look in memory lane, the past several thousand years, if the devil were in total control, we would have an entirely different world today. Because up to this date, he is still fighting to defeat the saints of God. Up to this day, he is trying to destroy the world and the Word of God, and they are very much here. That means Satan doesn't have the power that he wants us to believe he possesses.

God in Christ was given complete power and authority over the all the principalities and powers.

And ye are complete in him, which is the head of all principality and power:

It's a known fact to the principalities and powers that the children of God have unlimited power and authority in Christ. And it has to do with unwavering faith and obedience to God. They also know, if only they could influence us to believe lies concerning our faith, doubt, and be inconsistent with our prayer devotions, living and practicing the Word of God, we can indeed be defeated.

So to be made complete in Christ is absolute, full, and overflowing, with no ending, praise the Lord!

"In whom also ye circumcised with the circumcision made without hands." That means in Christ Jesus, the fleshly man has been stripped away, that the spiritual man can come forth. That's why we can express the life of God in our day-to-day walk. So we are able to minister the Word of God, pray, and live a holy, consecrated life before God. If the flesh has its way, we will certainly not be praying, certainly not be able to live the will of God, walking righteously. We would do precisely what the carnal man dictates, which is to sin and sin continually in rebellion against God.

So we are expressing that circumcised life, and it is walking in the spirit of God. "In putting off the body of the sin of the flesh, by the circumcision of Christ" (verse 11). We have a responsibility by putting away this sinful life that goes against total surrender to the will and purposes of God. We must be in control of our life and our destiny, and it's the choices that we must make.

Buried with Him in baptism—that is symbolic because of Jesus Christ's death, burial, resurrection, and ascension.

But your faith, when you believe in Jesus Christ, in a manner you are alike in a spiritual sense. That is a symbolic identity with His burial, and that is baptism, raised from the dead, which is lifting out of the water and being ascended on high, which is that relationship with Christ.

Embedded in faith with Him and now seated at the right hand of the Father in power and authority, wherefore also He has risen with Him through the faith of the operation of God. The action of God has to do with Jesus Christ's death, burial, resurrection, and ascension. Just by believing the whole process of the operation of Jesus Christ, you are quickened, made one with Him, come alive with Him, identify with Him, so when He's raised up, you are raised with Him. And you are dead in your sins and the uncircumcision of the flesh as He quickened together with Him having forgiven all your trespasses.

So God has forgiven you of all your sins and your many short-comings, failures, and your weaknesses. He has forgiven you, and Has given you the power to abstain from sin, to resist it, put it under your feet and to crush it.

We must! We must take that opportunity in doing it.

We as a people will always make mistakes, still committing sins because we have this human nature to contend and rebel against God.

Jesus Christ did not receive the blood of Adam. None of Adam's DNA was in Him, but we all are the seed of Adam and inherited the fallen state of Adam and must be contending with that state. With this fallen flesh, Jesus Christ has made it easy for us when He died for us. He took unto Himself all our sins and gave unto us His righteousness, the overcoming power to resist and say no!

And because he understood man's failures and man's weaknesses, His mercies extend beyond and above all we could ever think.

There is something we need to know. When Adam fell, man became sin, and God being perfect, with no knowledge and personal experience of sin had no idea what sin was or felt like. Only when the Son of Man became sin did God the Father experience and felt sin and it was painful to God. When Jesus Christ became sin for us, because of the love of God the Father for his Son Jesus Christ, all the mercies of God has extended beyond any sin that man could ever commit in order to bring man back onto Himself.

We serve a wise God, a God who loves us, with a love that He would do this great thing for us.

"And you, being dead in your sins and the uncircumcision of your flesh, hath he quickened together with him, having forgiven you all trespasses" (verse14). Blotting out the handwriting of ordinances that was against us, which was contrary to us, and took it out of the way, nailing it to His cross.

All the curses, all the evil pronunciations, all corruptions, anything that the enemy has on you, to condemn you, to make you feel guilty and feel bad, He took it all upon Himself; and not only that,

He blotted it out! Nullified it! Dismantled it! Canceled it! Satan now has nothing against us.

So what does the enemy and Satan do next? It is to accuse us. Anyone can blame you for anything. Even though it is not true, it can become true if you don't push back in God through prayer. Alternatively, the lie will become truth if it is continuously repeated, then you start to believe and accept it to be true.

In so doing we condemn ourselves, and the worst condemnation is for one to condemn oneself when no man condemns him. You put yourself in prison, and you will become your own slave master.

No one will be able to break you out of that psychological bondage when you put yourself there; only you can break yourself out because no man can know what's going on in your heart. No one can understand what's going on in your mind, but only you can break yourself free from that bondage by coming to and accepting the truth about yourself in the Word of God that whom the Son sets free is free indeed.

And having defeated all principalities and powers, He made a show of them, openly triumphing over them in it.

Jesus Christ is triumphant! He made a mockery of the devil and what he tried to do. The devil thought to himself that by crucifying the Son of Man, it would bring him victory over God and only too late he realized his mistake. The devil would not have permitted the Son of Man to be crucified and put to death if he realized it would result in his own defeat and demise. The foolishness of the cross is the wisdom of God.

If you should ever feel foolish when praying and calling on the name of Jesus Christ, and pleading the blood of Jesus Christ, imagine how foolish it seems to those who are looking at you yet have no understanding. It is the power of God, through deliverance and salvation, that empowers us to overcome the power of darkness.

Chapter 16

The Anointing and the Anointed

The Anointing of God

The anointing is the burden removing, yoke destroying Power of God. Jesus Christ is the embodiment of the anointing, empowered as the anointed one of God. We received the anointing through the Holy Spirit.

> However, the anointing which ye have received of him abided in you, and ye need not that any man teaches you: but as the same anointing teaches you of all things, and is the truth, and is no lie, and even as it hath taught you, ye shall abide in him. (1 John 2:27)

The anointing is within you; the Holy Spirit is the enabling power of God for you to do the things of God supernaturally. It's not you who does it; the Spirit of God gives you the ability to accomplish things.

The anointing teaches you all things. It inspires and gives you visions, revelations, and quick understanding. The Holy Spirit is the power of God that gives you the ability to do the will of God, makes all things known unto you, the things that you have a problem to understand by the Spirit of God. You will start realizing the most difficult things through revelation.

The anointing teaches, comforts, and empowers you to be a witness for Jesus Christ. It doesn't permit you to do worldly things, scam, or cheat, but only for the church, ministering the Gospel of Jesus Christ unto salvation for a full life with the hope of everlasting life with God.

So one must be anointed by God to have the anointing. When you have the anointing, it's tough and difficult for you to go against the will of God. He brings truth to bear and comes with firm conviction; meaning, your conscience will be your guide. "And even as it hath taught you, ye shall abide in him."

When you abide in something, you stay! You cannot be wavering or in conflict with your faith. You must know the Word of God because the anointing operates based upon the Word of God. You cannot desire the things of this world and the things of God at the same time because the anointing quickens your spirit, and you are now a witness of the Lord Jesus Christ.

> Is any sick among you? Let him call for the elders of the church; and let them pray over him, anointing him with oil in the name of the Lord: And the prayer of faith shall save the sick, and the Lord shall raise him. (James 5:14–15)

So the oil is symbolic and represents the anointing. When we pray over the oil, our prayer consecrates the oil and makes it holy unto the Lord. The oil is now symbolic of the anointing that represents the touch of the Holy Spirit.

The anointing breaks you and brings you to the point of submission. It melts you, chastises you with conviction, molds a new you, creates a clean heart and renews the right spirit within you. The anointing fills you, and empowers you for victory, wealth, and success.

Before a person can walk in the anointing power of God, it requires a strong zeal, love, and determination to do and accomplish the will of God by the leading of the Holy Spirit. The power of God rests upon the person of faith, enabling him to be a witness, a servant, for others unto Jesus Christ. No person by them self can walk in the anointing without being a servant of the Lord Jesus Christ.

You can know if a person is walking in the anointing because the anointing enables the fruits of the Holy Spirit such as love, peace, joy, contentment, patience, self-control. All these fruits have to do with the anointing. If you don't display those things in your daily life, if the anointing of God is not in you, you cannot be a representative of the kingdom life of Jesus Christ.

The Anointed of God

So many people confuse the anointed with the anointing. God can transform anyone or anything to be an anointed vessel, person, or thing to accomplish His will and purposes. God can anoint anyone or items, whether you are saved or unsaved, clean or unclean.

God can anoint a donkey to talk, or a rooster to relay a message, anoint a car, a house, a church. Any vessel can be anointed because the anointing can rest upon the person or the thing to make it holy and consecrated unto God. That doesn't mean that that person is sacred and consecrated but to fulfill the will of God

> Now he which established us with you in Christ,
> and hath anointed us, is God. (2 Corinthians 1:21)

God can choose any person, saved or unsaved, to fulfill His will and purposes. The anointing rests upon the anointed, God's chosen vessel to accomplish His will. He can choose to anoint an individual to be king, even if that individual is ungodly and unrighteous, for the purpose to be an anointed representative for Him to destroy and break down His enemies. It could be a particular kingdom He wants to destroy and uproot.

A pastor can be an anointed servant of God, living an unclean and unholy life, and still be doing the ministry of God and operating in the Spirit of God through souls saved, the message being preached and people in the church having their lives transformed. However, that pastor's life is a mess in the eyes of God. If he does not repent and seek forgiveness, there will be no place reserved for him in the kingdom of God.

> Many will say to me in that day, Lord, Lord, have we not prophesied in thy name? And in thy name have cast out devils? And in thy name done many wonderful works? And then will I profess unto them, I never knew you: depart from me, ye that work iniquity. (Matthew 7:22–23)
>
> Now know I that the LORD saved his anointed; he will hear him from his holy heaven with the saving strength of his right hand. (Psalm 20:6)

Whenever people who are anointed by God perform any type of action in line with their calling, their actions are not a result of their own power, but the Power of the Holy Spirit of God which empowers them. God will keep them safe and protect them from harm and danger.

Let's take a look at the life of Samson, who is known as the strongest man who ever lived in the bible. He was a Nazarite from birth, and his strength was a covenant God made with his parents, and his strength was his hair. He could do just about anything in power and the zeal of God. The day when he lost his hair, he lost his strength in God because the anointing was his strength that was placed upon him as the anointed vessel of God.

There was something important to learn from the life of Samson. The seven locks of hair upon the head of Samson was his strength from God. Samson's strength was also his weakness to God.

The Bible says, "Touch, not my anointed and do my servant no harm" (1 Chronicles 16:22).

Saul was a king, and he was anointed by Samuel to serve. He disobeyed and rebelled against God's instructions, and his heart turned from serving God. God rejected Saul from being king, but God still considered Saul as his anointed servant.

In 2 Samuel 1:14, David said unto the Amalekite, "Was thou not afraid to stretch forth thy hands to destroy the Lord's anointed?" The Amalekite came back and reported that he had killed Saul because the king requested to die because of his pain and agony from the injury he received in battle. Even though God rejected Saul, he was operating in the office of God as a king. God anointed him and appointed him to be king over the children of Israel. He was protected and covered until God chose to remove him as the king of Israel. God had him killed. He dismissed him by death.

So when God anoints a person, no one can replace him until he is dead.

So if you have a pastor in a church who is anointed by God to serve in the church, the anointing will never leave him until he is dead. Even if God rejects him, the anointing will still rest upon him. Not the anointing in him, the anointing upon him to do the will and purposes of God.

Being an anointed servant of God, the anointing can crush and destroy the soul if it does not operate according to the will of God, and when the work of God has been accomplished, the life of that person is terminated. Such a one would have already fulfilled their life's purpose depending on their calling.

There is a seasonal calling by God to fulfill a purpose. John the Baptist was anointed by God, and his assignment was to be the forerunner for Jesus Christ by preaching and baptizing until Christ's ministry began.

As soon as Christ was baptized, there was no need for the ministry of John the Baptist anymore; he became insignificant and useless because he had accomplished his purpose.

When the anointing is upon the anointed chosen one, such a one will be protected by God despite all what that soul does; they will be able to do great things even though their life may not line up with God. They are there for a purpose, and if anyone tried to destroy such a one that will represent the anointing upon his life, God will defend the anointing and will remove the one who seeks to destroy the one who carries the anointing.

Chapter 17

Understanding Your Dreams

We struggle at times to understand what dreams are about, and it becomes very much confusing because we are experiencing and feeling things while we are sleeping, and we don't know how to interpret or make any determination about what's happening.

We are more familiar with our daily surroundings of the things we see, hear, and touch, but unfamiliar with what's going on when we are asleep and dreaming.

It bugs our mind, the things we see and experience while we are sleeping that seem to be so real and what to make of some of these things that are revealed makes no sense, and it's confusing. Dreams are very much symbolic and need interpreting. A vision is an extension of a dream, and it has more clarity to it because God reveals Himself to us in visions than in dreams.

Also, Satan can manipulate our thoughts and our mind. He can implant things in our subconscious and cause us to experience what we are thinking, imagining, or dreaming that will affect us in many ways.

Many people dismiss dreams as nothing because they have no understanding of what it means because it makes no sense. So the more you understand what you're dreaming, the more you are able to deal with some of the most strange, questionable things that begin to appear and to happen in your life suddenly. Because most of the time, if not all the time, some of the things that we dream do come to pass, but we don't understand the symbolism associated with our dreams.

Pray for wisdom and a clearer understanding, to know how to interpret the things that you have dreamt, especially if it reveals something troubling and concerning. God speaks to us in dreams and visions, for instructions or to communicate a warning of pending dangers concerning the paths we take and the decisions we make.

> For God speak once, yea twice, yet man perceived
> it not. (Job 33:14)

When you're on a destructive path, God will talk to your heart through a person, things, or objects, dreams, and visions. God will interact with you by whatsoever medium He chooses to relate or communicate His message. It will directly connect with the past and present indulgence or experiences.

Communicating with you in dreams and visions is a way to derail the plan of the devil and your arrogance by revealing to you that God knows all your secrets and the traps put in place by the devil. He wants to steer you away from them.

When you think no one else knows your secrets because of your guilt, God will cause chastisement in your heart with heavy conviction. However, at times, we ignore the signs and warnings in whichever form it come.

> In a dream, in a vision of the night, when deep
> sleep falls upon men, in slumbering's upon the
> bed. (Job 33:15)

So God talks to us in dreams and makes it clear through visions because visions and dreams are similar. Visions are a more detailed extension of a dream and because there is greater clarity and awareness, appear to be more real.

Dreams can be personal in the form of a rebuke, a warning, or a guideline to awaken your spirit to be alert and aware.

Visions can also be a view or revelation of things that may not concern you personally. It has to do with something on a much broader scale and appears with symbols, signs, and weird characters, fictional story forms that is relatable to something close or familiar to you, to construct and depict something for you to contemplate and think on. Dreams, on the other hand, will decide your direction. It's something that would cause you to be terrified. It is best said in the following scripture:

> God scares me with dreams and terrifies me through visions. (Job 7:14)

Dreams come while you are sleeping, sometimes in your conscious or subconscious state. When you're in an unconscious state, you will not remember the dream that you are having.

When you are in a subconscious state, you will remember the dream with vague insight, but when you're in a conscious state while you're sleeping, you will remember the dreams in detail. Vision appears when you're partially awake, and an open vision is a revelation of things viewed while you are very much awake. The reason being is that dreams are spiritual. It has something to do with your spiritual man. We can never understand the fullness of the spiritual with our human brains.

However, we can interpret information from spiritual happenings and experiences through our conscience, our spiritual mind, commonly referred to as the heart. Our heart is like a processing center where all information, spiritual and environmental, are distributed to all five senses to interpret for the human understanding.

> A man's heart devises his way: but the Lord directed his steps. (Proverbs 16:9)
> Keep thy heart with all diligence; for out of it are the issues of life. (Proverbs 4:23)

When you are in a subconscious state, you're able to interpret spiritual revelations and encounters.

Prior to awakening, you will have and understand what you have seen and experienced in your dream and vision, to make some form of connection with the things that you have seen in your dream and with things that you are familiar with in your everyday life and activities.

> Then he opened the ears of men, and sealed their instruction. (Job 33:16)

God gives you directions while you're sleeping, so you would wake up in the morning with a new understanding based upon the dream that you were having.

So the thoughts that you have could be a direct result from your dream. A dream that you are unaware of can cause you to think about something that is now in your mind because it was placed there from a dream.

And it is an instruction guiding you down a particular path because when we get such dreams, we are always committing sin against God because we are not able to relate to Him through His word.

We are caught up doing so many things, and while we are sleeping, that's the way God talks to us.

> That he may withdraw man from his purpose and hide pride from man. (Job 33:17)

God wants to communicate with us because we are in sin and absent from the Word of God. The only time God speaks to us is when we are at peace and resting. He places the instructions in our heart so that we will take instructions and the guidance seriously.

Many times, when people have visions and dreams, they ignore it and consider it as foolishness because they can't make sense of the weird images. But this is the way God seals His instructions in our heart, to guide and direct us from the path of destruction, for man's intention is in his heart, desperate to do wickedness.

So if we have a plan to carry out sinful behaviors and activities, God will talk to us in various ways; and if we don't follow the warning signs and instructions from God, He will send His elect, our chosen ones, and speak to us directly as a final warning in a dream or vision.

> And for that the dream was doubled unto Pharaoh
> twice; it is because God establishes the thing, and
> God will shortly bring it to pass. (Genesis 41:32)

Anytime you have a dream and have a similar vision, this is God confirming something in your spirit to make known to you that it is essential. If you look back in your past, anytime you find yourself having the same dream twice, it is a confirmation of something that is about to happen. God is steering you away from danger; He wants to alert you, get your attention to something. Also, if you ask God for the revelation, God will make it known unto you.

Saul in his rebellion against God, killed all the prophets in Israel, therefore, there were no wise men of God left to counsel him in the right direction.

Saul became conflicted in his faith; he didn't know what to do. They are certain things in life that requires God's direct guidance to accomplish the task set before us. It's always good to have a spiritual person in your life to give you a word of wisdom, governed by biblical knowledge and understanding.

> Moreover, when Saul enquired of the Lord, the
> Lord answered him not, neither by dreams, nor
> by Urim, nor by prophets. (1 Samuel 28:6)

God answers our prayers in dreams, and many people dismiss dreams to be as foolishness without trying to understand the meaning of the dream and what it is saying to them. At times the Lord will give us dreams for important reasons.

> That he may withdraw man from his purpose
> and hide pride from man. (Job 33:17)

God is always watching over us, and the desire for us to do the right things. When we don't hear from God, it is for one out of two reasons. Either we are too close to Him or too far away from Him. A good well-behaved child's name will hardly be called, but an obscene misbehaving child's name will always appeal. If everything is going well in your relationship with God, your name will rarely be called because you're in fellowship.

Many good behaving Christians who desire to hear from God but are unable to hear Him will rarely have to be disciplined, but a disobedient misbehaving child will always have to be punished for bad behavior. These well-disciplined Christians won't hear His voice because there's no reason for Him to speak. God speaks when it is necessary to bring you in line on the path to righteousness. What God wants to do is to communicate His will to man in a relationship, and His communication with us comes in different ways, not only through hearing His voice. But with friendship and fellowship and embrace, you can feel the passionate love and warm embrace of God, like a baby in the arms of his mother.

When God speaks to us, He wants to save us from something that is disastrous, that we are unable to see for ourselves because we are so busy doing so many different things and confused by the number of distractions.

Even when the traps and snares are made known to us, it is suppressed and buried in our mind and heart because of unbelief.

People who are confused have many problems and are tormented. They always choose to be doing things with their hands, deliberately doing things to stay active, playing loud noise or music, love crowded places with excitement and any form of entertainments. This is to suppress frustrations, torments, guilt, and hurts from the constant tormenting voices repeating itself over and over in your head. To sit down for a moment, you will start to feel the guilts and shame. That will cause you to display the kinds of negative emotions that are tormenting you such as anger and frustration.

So many people can't sleep at night because they are tormented and afraid of their shadows to fall asleep because of the horrors that visit them while they are sleeping.

When God gives you a dream or vision, it never brings about torment. It tends to instruct, to guide, and empower you; to transform your life from one state to another. But when the enemy comes, he invades our dream with deception and false spiritual experiences with the intent to hurt, to harm, then to destroy by invoking fear, the most effective tool the devil uses to oppress God's people.

When we have dreams with no meaning, very confusing, not associated with anything, it comes to intimidate, confuse, and manipulate. You should have no choice but to rebuke it. Take authority over it because that dream is a seed sown in your soul.

When God reveals Himself to you in a dream, if you don't understand your goals, the Bible says that God will send an interpreter. "That he may withdraw man from his purpose and hide pride from man, God will send an interpreter."

> If there be a messenger with him, an interpreter,
> one among a thousand, to shew unto man his
> uprightness. (Job 33:23)

So you are very blessed when you have someone in your life who can interpret dreams or someone who is a messenger of God, a prophet to relate to you the things of God for empowerment.

Many people take things for granted. They are blessed and ignorant of their blessing. They have a messenger of God to interpret and make known clearly things they have no knowledge of, yet they ignore and take for granted God's servants.

If you're close to someone able to relate and make known to you the visions or dreams and their interpretations, that's a blessing. Many people live in this world; there is one in a thousand to be a blessing in your life. Be thankful to God.

Now if a person receives dreams and visions concerning a warning from God, and it has been interpreted by a messenger from God, take heed the chastening from God for God will deliver such a warning again and again. So dreams must be taken seriously because this is God's way of relating and communicating, inspiring and edifying His people to show them things that are present in their lives, things that are now happening and things that are about to happen to shape our future.

It all happens in visions and dreams, so when we have dreams and visions that we don't know, we should be praying to God for revelation, for understanding, for interpretation, that will lead to edification that will build us up in this Spirit of God for wise counsel and understanding: through understanding.

> And God came to Laban the Syrian in a dream
> by night, and said unto him, take heed that
> thou speak not to Jacob either good or bad.
> (Genesis 31:24)

God gives instructions in a dream the things that you ought to do and not to do, and we should take our dreams very seriously. You don't get dreams for no reason; you get dreams for a reason.

The devil tries to infiltrate our dream with various tactics to disguise himself as God, and many people are deceived by the dreams that they have because this is not God's way to say something else that appears in the dream to seduce and beguile.

How do you know that the dream is of God? If the dream bears no fruit, if the dream is not there to counsel; or to guide; to edify; empower; to encourage this is not of God.

However, if the dream is there to deceive, manipulate, create fear, cause conflict, or sow seeds of doubt in your mind concerning someone, then the dream is not from God, it is from the devil. Praise be to God!

About the Author

 Paul Barham, ordained as a pastor in July 2008, was called, trained, and anointed by God in the ministry of deliverance and spiritual warfare. He is the Pastor of a home church and operates a phone-line ministry. He was commissioned by God to write books and to teach and open the eyes of believers about the untold truths and mysteries in the Word of God. He explains what the body of Jesus Christ, represents in a simple and understandable way.

Born in Kingston, Jamaica, he grew up in a Christian home. His mother is an evangelist, and his father is an elder and founding member of the Redemption Church of God. Both parents have been associated with this church for nearly sixty years and they have been married for fifty eight years.

Pastor Paul was raised with one sister and three brothers in Bridge Port, Portmore, located in St. Catherine parish, Jamaica. He migrated to the United States in 2003 and currently resides in Naples, Florida with his family.

Paul Barham is married to Michelle Barham and they have four beautiful daughters.

CPSIA information can be obtained
at www.ICGtesting.com
Printed in the USA
LVHW031330081019
633523LV00003B/531/P